The Highly Sensitive Pe
practice advice for peo[...]
This proactive guide will help you take control of your environment, your relationships, and your emotions.

—Linda Johnsen, author of *Lost Masters*
and *A Thousand Suns*

The Highly Sensitive Person's Companion

Daily Exercises for Calming Your Senses in an Overstimulating World

TED ZEFF, PH.D.

New Harbinger Publications, Inc.

Publisher's Note

Distributed in Canada by Raincoast Books

Copyright © 2007 by Ted Zeff
　　　　　　　　New Harbinger Publications, Inc.
　　　　　　　　5674 Shattuck Avenue
　　　　　　　　Oakland, CA 94609
　　　　　　　　www.newharbinger.com

Cover and text design by Amy Shoup; Acquired by Jess O'Brien;
Edited by Carole Honeychurch

Library of Congress Cataloging-in-Publication Data

Zeff, Ted.
　The highly sensitive person's companion : daily exercises for calming your senses in an overstimulating world / Ted Zeff.
　　　p. cm.
　ISBN-13: 978-1-57224-493-1
　ISBN-10: 1-57224-493-3
　1. Sensitivity (Personality trait) 2. Self-actualization (Psychology) 3. Stress management. 4. Stress (Psychology) I. Title.
BF698.35.S47Z436 2007
155.2'32--dc22
　　　　　　　　　　　　　　　2006039644

10　　09　　08

10　9　8　7　6　5　4　3　2

Contents

The Five Senses

Stress Relievers

Diet

Exercise

Supplements

Relationships

Spirituality

Work

Soul

Conclusion

Acknowledgments

$\mathcal{I}$am grateful to Elaine Aron for being a beacon of light for highly sensitive people as she tirelessly continues to research, write, and speak on this topic that she developed. I am thankful to the many readers of *The Highly Sensitive Person's Survival Guide* who have encouraged me to write this book. I appreciate the editorial assistance of Adam Friend. I want to acknowledge Carole Honeychurch, my outstanding copyeditor, and Jess O'Brien, my acquisitions editor, for his unwavering support to see this project fulfilled. I am grateful to Eckhart Tolle, author of *The Power of Now* and *A New Earth*, for his inspiration in pointing the way to inner peace and truth. I am especially grateful to my spiritual teacher, Ammachi, who is the living embodiment of unconditional love and service, and who continues to inspire millions of people to awaken to their true divine nature within.

Introduction

$\mathcal{H}$ighly sensitive people make up approximately 20 percent of the population in every country. The HSP (highly sensitive person) is more aware of subtleties in the environment and can therefore be easily overwhelmed by noise, crowds, and time pressure. HSPs tend to be sensitive to pain, the effects of caffeine, and violent images and are also made uncomfortable by bright lights, strong scents, and changes in their lives.

Highly sensitive people have a finely tuned nervous system and need to create a balance in our fast-paced and aggressive society by taking care of themselves. HSPs tend to process sensory stimuli more deeply than most people. It can be both an enjoyable and a challenging trait to have.

In *The Highly Sensitive Person's Survival Guide*, I introduced hundreds of coping strategies to help HSPs survive in our overstimulating world. This companion book offers weekly exercises for the highly sensitive person to help you create more inner peace in your life. For those who have read *The Highly Sensitive Person's Survival Guide*, this is a good opportunity to review the coping techniques before you perform each exercise. For those not familiar with the first book, it's important to spend time reading each section in this companion book slowly as you thoroughly absorb the new material.

How to Use This Book

In this companion book, I present many inspirational exercises on how to live a harmonious life and thrive. There are fifty-two different areas for you to work on—one topic for each week during the year. It's best to complete just one exercise each week so that you will slowly be able to integrate the new technique into your life. However, feel free to spend more than a week on each topic if you'd like more time to make these necessary positive changes. Also, don't pressure yourself to complete all of the exercises. After reading the description of an exercise, sit quietly and contemplate whether you feel drawn to participate in the assignment. As an HSP, you are intuitive, and you'll know which exercises to partake in. Spend a few minutes thinking of what you want to write down before you begin an exercise. This book is just for you, so try not to judge your answers. Write down the information from your heart, as if you were writing in a diary or a journal. You may want to either type the answers on your computer or write in a notebook if that feels more comfortable.

Sharing some of the helpful hints with a close friend or partner is an excellent method for receiving support in implementing the positive changes you desire. After you complete an exercise, it will be helpful to begin listing the changes that you want to implement on your calendar or make a list of activities to work on during the week. The key to a happy life for the highly sensitive person is planning ahead. It's very important to make the necessary preparations to reduce stimulation in advance, such as taking earplugs or a headset with you when you are going into a noisy environment.

How the Book Is Arranged

The weekly exercises in this book are divided into thirteen different sections. In the first, you will learn how to change habits by investigating your beliefs, discarding false beliefs, and identifying stressors in your life and brainstorming possible solutions. In the next section, you will learn ways to raise your self-esteem by focusing on your positive HSP characteristics, observing how societal pressures influence you, and practicing how to inform others about your trait.

Next, you will learn how to develop a morning routine, including various physical exercises and meditations. Then you will create an evening routine by integrating calming activities into your life and creating a plan for better sleep. In the next section, you will learn various techniques to calm all five of your senses as well as take regular mini retreats.

The sixth section of the book teaches you to practice relaxation techniques to cope with the daily pressures of our fast-paced, overstimulating world. Then, you will learn how to create a new, calming diet for the highly sensitive person. Next, you will begin practicing specific physical exercises that fit the HSP temperament and learn how to implement a regular exercise routine. You will learn how to safely take the appropriate supplements, vitamins, and herbs as you gain a better understanding of medical care for the HSP.

In the tenth section, we will be exploring relationships and the HSP. You will learn new skills and complete innovative exercises to promote harmonious relationships in your life. Then you will learn how relationships can improve when you relate to others on a spiritual level and use visualization to heal wounds from the past.

The twelfth section teaches many techniques to create a peaceful work environment, including an exploration of how to create a new, stress-free job. And finally, you will gain an understanding of how developing a spiritual orientation helps the HSP and learn how to integrate spiritual experiences into your daily life.

Let's now begin the exciting adventure of creating a new, more peaceful life.

Your Belief System

$\mathcal{O}$ne of the keys to making positive changes in your life is to create an intention to release those habits that have caused you discomfort. Resolving to integrate new methods into your daily routine is paramount for success. Make a commitment now that you will spend the time and energy necessary to complete the following weekly exercises and integrate them into your life. As you begin implementing the suggestions in the book your joy level will increase and you will be even more motivated to change.

Let's first investigate how your belief system influences your thoughts, feelings, and behavior as an HSP. Most children were taught by their parents, teachers, peers, and the media that they can only be happy if they live a stimulating life based on outer gratification, such as making a lot of money, finding the perfect mate, and achieving success at work. Trying to obtain a feeling of self-worth exclusively from outside stimuli can create anxiety and tension for the reflective, sensitive person.

We all have been taught values by family, friends, teachers, and the media—values that have shaped our beliefs. For this exercise, concentrate on beliefs that you suspect are untrue for you or that may be making your daily life more difficult. List them. Make sure to take your time as you reflect on the values that you were taught as a child and how they were translated into ill-adaptive beliefs. Some examples are:

* I need to get good grades or I'm a failure.

* Unless I earn a good income, life will be difficult.

* I need a life partner or I will be miserable and lonely.

* It's dangerous to express my feelings.

* I should be a good athlete or people will think I'm not cool.

* If I don't dress well, people will think less of me.

* I shouldn't let anything bother me.

Review your list of beliefs. Which false beliefs have you internalized that you wish to discard? Put a check mark by them.

Now make a list of new beliefs that you would like to internalize. Some examples are:

* Real happiness comes from inner peace, not outer wealth.

✳ It's nurturing for my soul to express my emotions.

✳ Performing quiet activities is more enjoyable than always going out.

✳ I am happy to be single.

✳ When I close my eyes and feel peaceful energy flowing through my inner body, I know that I don't need outer stimulation to make me happy.

When you are experiencing any tension during the week, spend some time each day discovering if your stress is based on false beliefs that you have internalized from childhood. Make a conscious effort to let go of those old, worn-out beliefs and substitute them with new ones that value and promote inner peace for the highly sensitive person.

Making Changes in Your Life

*I*t's important to try to change any situation that creates stress in your life. Your home and work environments are the most important factors that determine your ability to create a peaceful life, so it's imperative that you do what you can to make them harmonious. Once you realize that a specific situation creates tension, try to change the stressful circumstances. If this is not possible, consider removing yourself from the source of tension.

What situations in your life are creating stress and tension? Some examples are:

✳ Too much noise at home in the evenings

✳ Violence in the media

✳ Pressure at work

❊ Noisy neighbors

❊ Having to go out a lot with my partner

Spend some time thinking of ways to change a challenging, stressful situation in your life. When changing habits, you need to be gentle with yourself and make the changes slowly. As you work through this book, you'll get many new ideas to help you resolve the current situation. But for now, just spend a few minutes brainstorming some possible solutions. Do you have any habits that tend to cause you stress? What new, nonstressful habits could you substitute? Write down as many ideas as you can. Some examples are:

❊ Reading

❊ Meditating

❊ Journal writing

❊ Drinking herb tea

❊ Taking walking breaks during the day at work

❊ Listening to relaxation tapes or CDs

In the following weeks you will slowly but surely release old habits that have created stress in your life. You are now ready and willing to embrace new, practical techniques that will create a life filled with peace and joy. This week, enjoy identifying and beginning to replace habits that cause you stress with new activities that create inner peace.

Glad to Be an HSP

As an HSP you have probably found it challenging to live in a society that values aggression and overstimulation. Since HSPs are a minority of the population, you may have internalized the values of our stimulating, non-HSP society. When you hold values that tend to negate what is true in your own life, you yourself may feel negated. This is a surefire recipe for low self-esteem.

Most people who remain in emotionally destructive situations do so because their low self-esteem tells them that they deserve to suffer. They don't value themselves because they believe that there is something wrong with them. Sometimes one's identity is based on suffering. HSPs can unconsciously be involved in emotionally destructive situations as they desperately try to maintain this fictitious identity. It's time to change the false belief that there is something wrong with you for being a highly sensitive person.

Your Positive Sensitive Traits

Although our trait can be challenging, some of the marvelous benefits of being an HSP include the following:

* We are conscientious and loyal.

* We have the capacity to deeply appreciate beauty, art, and music.

* We can really appreciate delicious food due to our sensitive taste buds and can deeply enjoy scents due to our sensitive olfactory trait.

* We are intuitive and tend to have deep spiritual experiences.

* We will notice potential danger sooner than non-HSPs, such as immediately feeling a tick crawling on our skin.

* We are very aware of safety issues and will be the first one to know how to exit a building in case of an emergency.

* We help create positive changes in the environment, such as creating restrictions on smoking, pollution, and noise.

* We advocate the humane treatment of animals.

❊ We tend to be kind, compassionate, and creative, making us natural counselors, teachers, and healers.

❊ We have an enthusiasm for life and experience love and joy more deeply than non-HSPs (when we aren't feeling overwhelmed).

Which of the above traits have you experienced in your life? Are there others?

Write down specific examples of how your sensitivity has manifested in positive ways in your life.

This week spend some time each day reviewing and appreciating your wonderful sensitive traits and adding to the list as you remember more specific examples of how your positive sensitive traits have manifested in your life.

As you come to appreciate your wonderful qualities as a highly sensitive person, your self-esteem will increase. When appropriate, try to share examples of your positive sensitive traits with your family, friends, and coworkers during the week.

An Out-of-Balance Society

$\mathcal{A}$nother way to raise your self-esteem is to realize that there is nothing wrong with you, but that we are living in a society that is out of balance. Overstimulation throughout the world has increased at an alarming rate in the last thirty years. It simply doesn't work for an HSP to try to fit into our aggressive, frenetic world.

Write down some of the ways that you feel that society has become out of balance and how this has affected you. Some examples are:

* Clogged freeways and road rage

* Huge, impersonal, overcrowded stores

* Increased violence in society like school shootings and vicious song lyrics

* Increased use of computers and cell phones

✳ A thousand television stations with a multitude of shows saturated with graphic sex and violence

Now imagine that you are living thirty or forty years ago. Write down the ways that that environment would have helped you to feel more peaceful. Some examples are:

✳ My commute to work doesn't take long.

✳ Nobody is answering the phone, so I'll try calling later (no answering machines, cell phones, or e-mails).

✳ My children are safe when they go to school.

✳ I enjoy going to the hardware store since the owner knows me by name.

As you come to realize how out of balance society has become, you may reconsider your efforts to adjust to the fast-paced, aggressive world. Spend some time each day this week contemplating why it is healthy for you not to try to conform to our overstimulating world. Discuss your new understanding with your family and friends.

Informing Others About Your Trait

$\mathcal{I}$t's likely that somewhere along the line, someone has told you that there is something wrong with you for being sensitive. So you'll feel prepared for the next time this happens, consider having a response ready.

You could tell the person, "According to research by Dr. Elaine Aron, HSPs are thought to make up approximately 20 percent of the population (equally divided between males and females). This population has a more finely tuned central nervous system, so we are more susceptible to both positive and negative environmental stimuli. The stimuli could be noise, fragrance, certain foods, chaos, beauty, or pain. We tend to process sensory stimuli more deeply than most people. It can be both an enjoyable and a challenging trait to have."

Write down in your own words a description of your trait. After you're done, memorize this explanation and practice telling one person each day this week about your trait. You may want to role-play with a family member or trusted friend before telling someone at work, a neighbor, or an acquaintance about your trait. You could also practice in front of a mirror.

One note of caution is that it's important to use discretion regarding with whom you share your trait. If you think the other person would ridicule or discount your sensitivity, it's best not to open up to them. Sometimes an insensitive family member or coworker may disregard your description of highly sensitive people, which could actually make you feel worse.

Morning Exercise and Meditation

*W*hile you can't live your life in a glass bubble, removed from the world's overstimulation, you can create an environment that minimizes stimuli. An important step in reducing stimulation for the HSP is to create a morning routine. This structure will help you feel more centered throughout the day. By waking up only twenty minutes earlier and performing calming activities, you can begin your day in a peaceful state. Then you will be better prepared to handle stimuli throughout the day.

Exercise

It's good to do some physical activity when you first awaken. This has an energizing effect on the body. But remember to check with your doctor before starting any exercise program.

What physical activity would you like to do to begin your day this week? Some examples are:

* Gentle stretching

* Hatha yoga

* Tai chi

* Walking in place

* Vigorous activities, such as sit-ups or push-ups performed slowly, with concentration

Begin each day this week by spending a few minutes trying the physical activity that you feel most drawn to. To help you remember this new step in your routine, you can put a note on your night table or on your bathroom mirror.

Meditations

Once you have completed some physical activity, it's important to do at least fifteen minutes of some type of meditative practice. Various meditation practices are described in the next few pages. This week, just begin doing the deep-breathing exercise listed below. You may want to record some of the later guided meditations that you will be using during the next four weeks. You could also have a partner or friend read the visualization to you.

Deep-Breathing Exercise

*Sit in a comfortable position and close your eyes. Inhale
slowly through your nose into your abdomen to the count
of five ... hold to the count of five ... and slowly exhale
to the count of five... Feel your body becoming more and
more relaxed with each exhalation...*

*Repeat the slow, deep breathing exercise again...
Really experience how calm and peaceful your body feels
with each exhalation... Just observe the thoughts when
they arise ... then calmly return to your breathing...
Inhale peace and calmness ... hold ... exhale any
stress...*

During the breathing exercise you can mentally repeat a
mantra, such as the word "peace" or "calm," with each inhalation and each exhalation. You may find it more comfortable to
inhale to a count of less than five seconds. Arrange the timing
of the breath so that it feels comfortable to you. While you are
watching your breath or repeating a mantra, you will begin to
feel calm in the present moment rather than identifying with
the myriad of anxious thoughts running through your mind.

Remind Yourself

One effective method of motivating yourself to begin your
daily routine is to note on your calendar every day this week

to set your alarm to get up twenty minutes earlier. Keep this appointment just like you would a doctor's appointment. You are becoming your own healer, so set your alarm and realize that this simple morning practice will create more inner peace and joy throughout your day.

Progressive Relaxation

*N*ow that you are familiar with the deep-breathing exercise, you can begin doing progressive relaxation, which consists of relaxing all the muscles in your body while taking slow, deep breaths. Try the following exercise every day this week and notice how peaceful you feel at the end of the visualization. You can tape-record it to make using it easier.

>*Focus your attention at the top of your head as you feel your scalp relaxing … if your jaw is clenched, just open your mouth slightly and relax your jaw… Your eyes are relaxing … your facial muscles … your lips … your cheeks are all now very relaxed … take a long, deep breath … hold … and slowly exhale as your neck becomes looser and looser…*
>
>*Relax your shoulders… Feel any weight that you've been carrying around easily evaporate as your shoulders*

*become so loose and free … you may want to gently
rotate your shoulders…*

*Feel a warm tingling flow of energy slowly move
down your right upper arm … to your right forearm …
and through your right hand to your fingers … recognize
how good it feels to release the tension from your head,
neck, shoulder, and arm and feel it flow out through your
fingertips… Now have that same energy flowing down
your left upper arm … through your left forearm … into
your hand … as the tension flows out of the tips of your
fingers…*

*Remember, when a thought comes, just observe it
and return to your breathing… Now feel your chest
deeply relaxing… Your stomach is loose as your abdomen
rises with each inhalation and deflates with each
exhalation…*

*Visualize your upper back being gently massaged as
all the muscles relax deeper and deeper… Now your mid
back… And now your lower back… Really feel the back
muscles relax more and more with each exhalation…*

*Feel your buttocks relaxing … let go of all tension
in your right thigh … right knee … and now the right
calf… Visualize your right foot being gently massaged as
all the tension from your right leg flows out through the
sole of your right foot…*

*Breathe slowly and consciously … as you begin to
relax your left thigh … left knee … left calf … feel your*

left foot also being massaged as all the tension from your left leg is flowing out through the sole of your left foot…

Your entire body is now relaxing further as you dive deeper and deeper into a blissful state … each and every cell in your body feels warm and peaceful…

Now visualize yourself in a tranquil scene in nature… You may be in the mountains … or by the ocean … or at a river bank… Notice the magnificent colors of the flowers … the lush green of the trees … and the sparkling blue water… Clearly see this beautiful natural environment… What other beautiful sights are you gazing at?…

What sounds do you hear?… Melodic chirping of birds?… The flow of the water?… Feel the gentle warmth of the sun on your body as you lie in the soft grass or sand… Can you smell the sweet fragrance of flowers?… The scent of the ocean or fresh mountain air?…

Remain in this pastoral setting for as long as you like and whenever you're ready, slowly open your eyes and tell yourself to take this deep feeling of inner peace and joy with you throughout the day.

Please note that most of these visualizations are recorded on the CD "The Highly Sensitive Person's Healing Program." (For more information about the HSP healing CD, please visit www.hspsurvival.com.)

Centering Meditation

*S*ince HSPs are so easily affected by other people's moods, it's important to practice grounding techniques. This week we are going to learn an effective centering visualization that would be beneficial to try each morning this week.

Sit in a comfortable position with your eyes closed…
Once you have completed a few minutes of slow, deep
breathing, imagine that a soft, flexible green cord is
attached to the base of your spine… Clearly observe
this cord… The cord is slowly moving from your spine
toward the floor… Imagine two more green cords that
are attached to the soles of your feet… Now visualize
all three green cords meeting at the Earth's surface and
forming one large, strong green cord…

Observe the large green cord as gravity pulls the thick
rope deeper toward the center of the Earth… The cable

is now traveling through layers and layers of solid rock ... deeper and deeper... You can clearly see the cord traveling as it slowly moves toward the center of the Earth...

Finally, the green cord arrives at the very center of the Earth... The rope anchors itself to the Earth's center, and you begin to slowly inhale calm, centered, and stable energy from the Earth's core... Visualize the energy slowly rising toward the Earth's surface with each inhalation...

The energy easily ascends toward the ground level... Observe the grounding energy arrive at the Earth's surface... The powerful energy ascends through the floor and into the soles of your feet... You feel the energy rising up your legs... You feel solid and centered like a rock...

Now feel the Earth's energy enter the base of your spine... The serene, grounded energy feels so soothing... Feel this Earth energy slowly travel up your spine and through your lower back ... mid back ... upper back ... neck ... all the way to the top of your head... You feel centered, calm, and strong as this core energy circulates throughout your entire being ... filling every cell of your body... Breathe in the Earth's energy for a few moments... You are calm, centered, and happy... You are calm, centered, and happy... You are calm, centered, and happy.

You may also want to use this visualization any time throughout the day, especially when being negatively affected by other people.

White Light Meditation

*A*nother method to protect yourself from negative energy is to visualize a white light surrounding your body. This is an effective technique to utilize in the morning to center yourself or before entering a room with a large group of people. Try practicing this visualization and observe if you feel calmer after interacting with other people.

> *Once you have completed a few minutes of slow,*
> *deep breathing, visualize a crystal-clear white light*
> *encircling your body… Notice how the shimmering light*
> *encompasses every inch of your skin… Observe clearly*
> *how strong the shield is… Imagine negative energy*
> *bouncing off the impenetrable armor and ricocheting*
> *back to its source… You are safe and protected… You*
> *are safe and protected… You are safe and protected…*

When performing these meditative exercises, it's natural for the mind to come up with negative thoughts about the past or future. As soon as you become aware of a negative thought arising in the mind, the thought loses its power over you as you simply return to your meditation.

While meditation is an ideal way to center yourself in the morning, it's important to do whatever relaxation exercise nourishes your soul. You may find that praying, writing, or self-reflection has a soothing effect on your nervous system. Some HSPs prefer to start the day reading a spiritually uplifting book.

Choose a method to center yourself, and practice it each morning this week upon awaking. You may want to try a different technique each day or use the same practice every morning. Some examples are:

* Deep-breathing exercise

* Progressive relaxation

* Centering meditation

* White light meditation

* Prayer

* Writing

* Self-reflection

* Reading a spiritually uplifting book

* Other type of meditation

By implementing a morning routine this week, you will set the groundwork for centering yourself every morning for the rest of your life!

After your morning relaxation routine, it's important for you to eat a nourishing breakfast slowly and leave plenty of time for your commute to work. It's beneficial to arise at the same time on weekends as you do during the week so that you'll be sleepy early on Sunday evening and your sleep biorhythms will remain regular.

Releasing Stress at Night

While following a morning routine is important for the highly sensitive person, developing an evening routine is equally valuable since it will help you release the stress of the day and promote better sleep.

It's important to do relaxing activities in the evening such as engaging in calm discussions and reading nonstimulating books before bedtime. Try not to watch stimulating television shows or movies or surf the Internet at night. It's important for HSPs to eliminate the negative media influences from their lives, especially in the evening. At least thirty minutes before going to bed, let go of the day by going inward.

Calming Activities in the Evening

The evening is an excellent time for performing one of the meditation techniques that you have practiced during the last few weeks. You may also want to listen to calming music or a relaxation tape or CD. It's important not to engage in stimulating activities during the evening in order to calm down your nervous system.

What are some calming activities that you would like to do in the evening? Each night this week, at least thirty minutes before bedtime, partake in something truly relaxing. Some examples are:

❊ Read an uplifting book.

❊ Write affirmations or write in a diary.

❊ Meditate wearing earplugs or a headset.

❊ Perform progressive relaxation.

❊ Take a warm bath with Epsom salts or essential oil of lavender.

❊ Listen to calming music or a relaxation tape or CD.

❊ Drink some chamomile tea.

❊ Massage yourself with soothing oils.

Just as you made a note on your calendar to create a morning routine, make an appointment with yourself every night this week to engage in calming activities at least thirty minutes before bedtime.

Sleep Problems

$\mathcal{D}$ue to your sensitivity to stimuli and difficulty relaxing after experiencing overstimulation, you may experience challenges in being able to get a good night's sleep. In my research based on questionnaires that my HSP students completed, I found that many HSPs have problems falling or staying asleep. If your insomnia is not due to physiological causes, your finely tuned central nervous system is probably the major component that inhibits a restful sleep.

When we experience overstimulation, stress hormones can activate our central nervous system. We become habituated to increased muscle tension, heart rate, and blood pressure as well as heightened sensory acuity. All these factors affect the quality of our sleep and promote insomnia.

Going to Bed Early

The optimal time to go to bed is by 10 P.M. It's easier to fall asleep before 10 P.M. due to the natural biorhythms of the day, and it's frequently more difficult to fall asleep closer to midnight.

What time do you go to sleep? If you go to bed after 10 P.M., write down what activities prevent you from going to bed earlier.

What changes can you make to go to bed earlier? Some examples are:

* Turning off the TV earlier in the evening

* Putting the kids to sleep earlier

* Avoiding late-night conversations with family members

Try going to bed an hour earlier this week if possible and notice if you have an easier time falling and staying asleep.

Don't Look at the Clock

One of the most important rules to follow to reduce sleep problems is never, ever look at a clock or watch after 8 P.M. Many of my students have had amazing success in stopping their insomniac pattern by just following this simple rule. The mind needs a negative hook to perpetuate sleep problems, and one of the best cues to create a sleep disorder is to look at the clock and worry about not getting enough sleep. When eight o'clock rolls around, stop looking at your clock and wait for what feels like about an hour. Then begin your calming evening routine and turn in.

This week, try not to look at a clock or watch after 8 P.M. How can you implement this effective technique? Some examples are:

* ❋ Turn my clocks around.

* ❋ Ask for support from my family members.

* ❋ Set my alarm clock for the morning before 8 P.M.

If you perpetually check the time, this technique may feel uncomfortable at first. However, once you employ this method for a few weeks, you will feel so peaceful and your sleep will improve so much that you won't want to ever look at a clock during the night.

Sleep Disturbances from Your Partner

If your partner is a restless sleeper, snores loudly, or wakes you up, you need to create a solution to this problem.

How can you resolve sleep problems with your partner? Some examples are:

* ❋ Use earplugs, a white-noise machine, or a fan.

* ❋ Listen to calming music (possibly with earbuds).

* ❋ Sleep in twin beds.

✳ Consider sleeping in separate bedrooms.

✳ Meet with a marriage counselor.

If your partner is a non-HSP who can fall asleep easily, you need to inform them how important it is for you to create a quiet environment in order to get a good night's sleep and ask for their cooperation.

Tips for a Good Night's Sleep

$\mathcal{W}$e discussed in week 4 that we have to disengage from our fast-paced, overstimulating world to experience inner peace. A hundred years ago people rarely experienced insomnia since most people lived in small towns or rural areas and were attuned to the peace and harmony of nature.

Turning Off Electronic Equipment

One way we can tune out some of the invasive modern stimulation and get back to a more peaceful, natural state is to simply turn off some of our technology.

What electronic equipment can you turn off every evening this week? Some examples are:

* Cell phone/pager

✳ Television and radio

✳ Computer

✳ The volume on the answering machine

✳ DVD player

After 8 P.M., turn off your electronic equipment and enjoy the serenity of living in a more natural environment.

Creating Gratefulness in Your Life

If you find yourself ruminating on a specific problem in the evening, spend up to an hour, if necessary, writing down every possible solution to the dilemma. Afterwards, realize that if you spend any more time thinking about the situation, it will not help you one iota in solving the problem. So just let it go. Finally, spend some time writing down everything that you're grateful for in your life so that you can go to sleep in a positive, stress-free state. Remember that your mind may have become attached to focusing on problems. When a negative thought arises, you may want to calmly observe that it's just the restless mind, and then return to your peaceful, optimistic state.

If you're thinking a lot about a specific problem this week, write down solutions to the problem in the evening.

Now write down everything that you're grateful for in your life. Remember that millions of people on the planet aren't able to meet the basic needs of food or shelter and have no access to medical assistance. Some examples of things to be grateful for are:

* My health

* My family

* My friends

* Enough food to eat

* A nice house

* The ability to work and earn money

* The chance to enjoy my hobbies

As you begin to focus on the joys in your life, you will need to let go of the belief that you must worry about your problems.

Creating a Nurturing Bedroom

To reduce overstimulation, your bedroom should be a quiet, dark, and safe space. A sense of serenity is increased by soft colors such as white, light blue, and light green. It's easier to fall asleep when your room is cool so that the body will not become overheated. It's best not to be exposed to bright light before going to sleep since the light can create wakefulness.

What changes can you make in your bedroom this week that will help you feel more tranquil in the evening and sleep better? Some examples are:

* I'll keep the temperature in my bedroom below 68 degrees.

* I plan to use earplugs and a white-noise machine, fan, or air purifier to drown out startling noises.

* I'll buy some heavy drapes to block out light from outside.

* I'll try using an eye mask.

* I'll buy a night-light.

* I plan to install a dead-bolt lock.

* I'll shop for a picture of a natural setting, like Monet's *Water Lilies*, for my bedroom.

As you create a tranquil environment in the evening by turning off electronic equipment, letting go of worries, and creating a nurturing bedroom, you will deeply soothe your central nervous system.

How Exercise, Diet, and Herbs Affect Sleep

Exercise

When you exercise, your body releases endorphins that actually reduce stress, promoting better sleep. A lack of physical exercise can also contribute to insomnia by inhibiting the daily rise and fall of body temperature. Exercise raises body temperature, which is followed by a drop three hours later, promoting sleep. It's not good to do aerobic exercise in the evening because the body needs about three hours to cool down. If you want to exercise in the early evening you can go for a slow walk or do some gentle yoga postures.

What type of exercise do you regularly perform and at what time? If you exercise in the evening, try to perform your physical activity before 6 P.M.

Diet

Since it takes two to three hours to digest a meal, late-night dinners could contribute to insomnia. Having a snack of some complex carbohydrates, such as a piece of whole-grain bread or some rye crackers, before bedtime can increase serotonin, a brain neurotransmitter that may induce sleep.

Foods that are heavy, warm, and moist are grounding and may help promote sleep. This kind of diet is both nurturing and centering, especially in the winter. Minimizing the use of caffeinated foods and beverages, such as coffee, black tea, chocolate, and soft drinks, will reduce stimulation and help you sleep better.

What time do you eat dinner? Try to eat dinner this week three hours before bedtime.

What are some heavy, warm, moist foods that you can eat this week? Some examples are:

✻ Soups

✻ Casseroles

✻ Lasagna

✻ Stew

Do you ingest any products that contain caffeine? If you do, list methods of reducing your intake. Some examples are:

* Adding a little more milk or nondairy creamer to my coffee each day

* Asking my friends or relatives for support to minimize caffeine usage

* Drinking herb tea instead of black tea or coffee

* Giving up soft drinks that contain caffeine

Herbs for Sleep

Taking some mild herbs a half hour before bedtime may help induce sleep. You may want to take an herbal formula containing a mixture of various calming herbs such as valerian root, passionflower, hops, kava kava, or skullcap. However, if you take herbs every night, your body can develop a tolerance, just like it does with sleeping pills. It's best to use herbs only when you need them, not every night.

List specific actions that you will take this week to learn about calming herbs that promote sleep. Some examples are:

* I will visit Web sites about herbs for sleep.

* I can research books by such well-known holistic medical doctors as Deepak Chopra and Andrew Weil.

✳ I will visit my local health-food store to obtain information about herbs for sleep.

As you begin a schedule of daytime exercise, eat a diet that is grounding and calming, reduce caffeine, and occasionally take some mild herbs, your sleep will improve this week.

Developing Positive Thoughts About Sleep

$\mathcal{O}$ne of the most important rules of improving your sleep is to develop a positive attitude. Negative thoughts about sleep can create a self-fulfilling prophecy that increases insomnia. It will be helpful to reframe any negative thinking into positive thoughts about sleep. It's important not to believe the fearful, untrue thoughts about sleep that arise in your mind.

List some negative thoughts you've had when you can't fall asleep. Some examples are:

"I have a busy day at work tomorrow, and I'll never be able to function on the job without sleep. I'll have to drink a lot of coffee to be alert at work; but then I'll get so nervous I won't be able to sleep tomorrow night."

"Oh no! It's 1 A.M. and I still can't fall asleep... Now it's 3:00, and I have to get up in exactly three hours, and I still haven't gotten any sleep. I'll be a wreck tomorrow."

"I hope I can fall back to sleep. I wonder what time it is. What? It's only 2 A.M.? That means I've only slept for three hours. I'll never be able to fall back asleep!"

Now replace your negative statements with new, positive statements that will calm down your nervous system. Some examples are:

"As long as I get my core sleep of about five and a half hours, I'll be fine at work. I can always take a short nap if I'm sleepy, which will help me feel alert. I'm not going to try to fall asleep. I'm just going to meditate and relax my muscles as I breathe slowly and deeply. Meditation is equivalent to light sleep, so I'll be fine tomorrow."

"I still have plenty of time to fall asleep. I've gone with a lot less sleep for one night without any difficulty. I don't need eight hours of sleep to function."

"Since I'm now going to bed by 10 P.M., I have many hours to relax in bed, and I'll still have plenty of time to get my core sleep. My goal isn't to fall asleep right away but just to spend some time enjoying relaxation by meditating or reading before going to sleep. When I'm drowsy later on, I'll fall asleep."

"I'm awake now, but I'm not going to worry about falling back to sleep. It's probably almost dawn, and I've had my core sleep of five and a half hours, so it doesn't matter if I fall back to sleep or not. I'll just enjoy relaxing for a while."

Remember that the mind needs a negative hook to perpetuate sleep problems and one of the best cues to create insomnia is to believe fearful, untrue thoughts about your sleep. As you reframe your thoughts about sleep this week, you will be using the power of your mind to heal your insomnia.

Traveling

Traveling may create sleep challenges for the HSP, so take the necessary sleep aids with you. Make sure that the room you're staying in is quiet, dark, safe, and at a comfortable temperature.

List some sleep aids that you can take on your next trip. You may want to keep the list in a convenient location (like next to your suitcase). Some examples are:

* A white-noise machine

* Earplugs

* An herbal remedy

* A relaxing book

* A flashlight (for reading)

❋ A night-light

❋ Allopathic sleeping pills (conventional medicines prescribed by your doctor or bought over the counter that you take only for a few nights, maximum)

❋ Calming medicated oil

❋ A small pillow filled with calming herbs like lavender

❋ Chamomile tea and a thermos

❋ A sleep mask

❋ A headset with a CD or tape of calming music or a recorded meditation

❋ Clothespins to make sure the drapes in the room don't let in light

Now that you know what to take with you on a trip to help you sleep well, you can confidently make plans to go on that trip you had been worried about. Bon voyage!

WEEK

15

Soothing Sights and Sounds

$\mathcal{I}$n the last few weeks you have developed a daily routine to deal with our overstimulating world. In the next few weeks you will learn techniques for calming the senses. By employing specific calming methods for each of the five senses—hearing, touching, sight, taste, and smell—you will be able to easily cope with overstimulation.

Hearing

In our noise-saturated society, hearing is the sense that can probably create the most challenges for the HSP. What with the advent of the now-ubiquitous cell phone (with people loudly talking into them in public venues), loud music blaring from powerful car speakers and your neighbor's home, barking dogs, leaf blowers, and lawn mowers, the sensitive person can feel trapped in a nervous net of noise with no escape. The cumulative effect of such grating sounds can wreak havoc for the HSP.

Make a list of the noises that disturb you in your daily environment. Some examples are:

※ Family members watching television loudly

※ People talking on cell phones

※ Noisy restaurants

※ Loud motorcycles, buses, and trucks driving by my home or office

※ Barking dogs

※ My neighbor's power tools

List specific techniques that you will employ this week to reduce noise in each of the areas that cause you stress. Some examples are:

※ I can play soft music in the background.

※ I will listen to a calming tape or CD on a headset.

※ I plan to use a white-noise machine, fan, or air purifier to mask jarring noises.

※ I will wear earplugs, an earmuff-style headset (like construction workers use), or a noise-canceling headset.

※ I will make an appointment with an audiologist to order a custom-made set of earplugs.

✳ I'll ask household members to use a headset when watching TV or to turn the sound down.

✳ I will look into soundproofing my home or office.

✳ I will purchase double-paned windows or heavy drapes.

✳ I will visit Web sites such as www.nonoise.org and www .noisefree.org to learn new methods to cope with noise.

✳ I'll consider moving if the noise at home can't be reduced.

As you begin implementing your personal noise-abatement plan this week, you will no longer be a victim of our out-of-balance, noise-saturated world.

Seeing

By constantly receiving excessive stimuli through your eyes, you are directly overloading your nervous system, creating anxiety and tension. When you do visualizations or meditations with your eyes closed, you will be able to dive deeply into the divine peace that lies dormant within your inner body.

Spend a few minutes thinking about what you spend most of your time looking at during the day. Does this particular visual stimulation cause you tension? Some examples are:

✳ A computer screen

✳ A television screen

* Very bright light

* An urban landscape

* Bright colors

Now create a list of changes that you can make this week to reduce tension from eyestrain. Some examples are:

* I will spend less time on the Internet and watching television.

* I will buy some large pictures of calming nature scenes for my home and office.

* I'll go shopping for clothes with calming colors like white, blue, and green.

* I can stop wearing clothes in stimulating colors like bright orange, yellow, and red.

* I will wear my sunglasses when I go outside.

* I will go for a walk in a park or other natural setting every day.

* I plan to take frequent meditation breaks when working at my computer.

Rather than letting excessive visual stimuli bother you this week, plan ahead by incorporating new methods to reduce the negative effects of sight on your nervous system.

Smelling and Touching

Eliminating Offensive Odors

Many HSPs are sensitive to odors. Some of us get headaches or allergic reactions when inhaling certain scents. Other highly sensitive people have reported that being near anyone who has on perfume can cause them to become nauseated. Make sure that your house and workplace are free of any noxious fumes.

Though this sensitivity can be challenging, it can also be beneficial, particularly in helping to calm down the nervous system. Aromatherapy is a branch of herbal medicine that uses essential oils extracted from plants and herbs to calm and give users a sense of well-being. If you can tolerate the aromas, inhaling the fragrances of certain oils, such as lavender, jasmine, and rose, can alter the brain waves, producing calmness and relaxation.

What odors in your environment are uncomfortable for you? Some examples are:

* Odors from dogs or cats

* Gasoline when I fill my car

* Stale and moldy odors at home and at the office

* Sitting near anyone wearing perfume

* The smell of magic markers and incense

How can you reduce exposure to noxious odors? Some examples are:

* I will use an air purifier or open the window to release stale smells at home.

* I can check to make sure my heating/air-conditioning system is working properly.

* I'll go to a health-food store and buy an aromatherapy kit.

* I will buy natural cleaning products for home and at work.

* I will wear a face mask whenever I have to go into a polluted environment.

* Whenever I am near someone wearing perfume, I will immediately move.

It's important for the HSP to plan ahead to avoid contact with any noxious odors. This week, spend some time creating a healthy, odor-free home and work environment.

Touching

An excellent method to soothe your nervous system is to receive a gentle massage. However, some sensitive people may find that a massage is too invasive. It's crucial for you to constantly give feedback to the massage therapist as to the degree of pressure that feels comfortable. Due to your characteristic openness, you may easily absorb the energy of the massage therapist, so be sure to interview the therapist before agreeing to a massage. Since some HSPs may not feel comfortable being touched by strangers, they may benefit more from receiving a massage from a partner or a close friend. Another excellent option is to massage yourself to release the stress from the day.

Try doing the following exercise several times a day during the week. Spend a few minutes with your eyes closed observing where you are holding tension in the body and then relax the tense areas through either gentle massage or relaxing the muscles.

✳ Do your shoulders feel tight?

✳ Are your legs or stomach tense?

✳ Is your jaw clenched?

❋ Are your hands clenched or are they loose?

❋ Where else are you holding tension in your body?

❋ Is your breathing shallow?

You may also want to try the following exercise several times a day. Focus your attention on your right hand for a few moments and feel the energy within the hand. Next focus your attention on the left hand for some time and feel the aliveness in that hand. Then feel the energy in both hands at the same time. Next visualize other parts of your body where there is tension and feel the energy within soothing that body area.

What techniques do you want to employ this week to soothe your tense body? Some examples are:

❋ I'll make an appointment with a massage therapist.

❋ I plan to ask my partner to trade massages with me.

❋ I'll enjoy giving more hugs each day this week.

❋ I plan to gently massage my body with warm sesame oil.

❋ I look forward to applying medicated sesame oil to my forehead at bedtime.

❋ I'll purchase an electric handheld massage wand or massage chair cushion.

❋ I'll consciously relax my tense muscles throughout the day.

✳ I plan to focus on the energy within my hands and then on any areas of tension in my body.

Just as nerve receptors in your nose can alter brain-wave patterns when stimulated by a pleasant aroma, the thousands of nerve cells in your skin can promote calmness and relaxation through touch.

Food and Drink

Some HSPs are sensitive to consuming hot or cold food and beverages. It's generally better to consume warm drinks and foods rather than those that are piping hot. Warm foods can calm your nervous system. Sometimes a cold raw-food diet (particularly in the winter) can increase anxiety and tension.

You may sometimes have difficulty consuming frozen foods such as ice cream. Ice-cold frozen desserts can sometimes cause headaches in sensitive people, so it's best to let any frozen treat melt in your mouth slowly.

It's important to drink lots of pure water daily to flush your system of toxins. Drinking a cup of herb tea, such as chamomile, can calm the nervous system. Minimizing coffee, black tea, and caffeinated soft drinks may reduce your anxiety. While some people find drinking alcohol relaxing, other highly sensitive people actually have an adverse reaction to even one alcoholic drink.

Make a list of the foods and drinks that you consume that may have a deleterious effect on your nervous system. Try to reduce or eliminate those products this week. Some examples may be:

* Ice-cold foods and ice water (especially in the winter)

* Very hot food and drinks

* Caffeinated soft drinks, black tea, and coffee

* Very spicy foods

* Sugar

* Preservatives

* MSG

What new foods and drinks do you want to begin using this week to help calm down your nervous system? Some examples are:

* Hot cereal

* Hearty soups

* Casseroles

* Warm milk

* Chamomile tea

* Soft drinks without caffeine

As you begin eliminating certain foods and drinks this week, be aware of the effect that these changes have on your nervous system. Do soothing, warm foods and drinks make you feel nourished and calm?

Taking a Regular Mini Retreat

As I wrote in *The Highly Sensitive Person's Survival Guide*, since you are sensitive to stimuli and are easily overwhelmed, it's important that you take a mini retreat at least twice a week. You can set aside a few hours one day during the week and a few hours on the weekend for nurturing yourself.

Inform your family or housemates that you need some quiet time when you won't be disturbed. If this is not possible in your home, try to find another place to nurture yourself. Do you have a friend, relative, or coworker who would be willing to offer their home to you for a few hours during the week?

The first step in creating your mini retreat is to turn off your phones and other electronic equipment and make sure that you're not disturbed by any outside stimuli, especially members of your household. If it's difficult to create a silent environment, create a noise-free atmosphere by playing some calming music, turning on a white-noise machine, or wearing earplugs. Now's the time to relax in bed or on your couch and read that spiritually uplifting book you never seem to get to, or just take a refreshing nap.

If you enjoy aromatherapy, put some calming essential oils in a potpourri pot or light incense or a scented candle. Make yourself a cup of chamomile tea. Prepare a special healthy snack (preferably without sugar) and spend some time really noticing the taste of each scrumptious morsel that you eat. Try closing your eyes and concentrating on the delicious taste on your tongue.

Next, try practicing some spiritually uplifting exercise such as hatha yoga or tai chi. You may want to purchase a yoga or tai chi DVD or videotape. Another option is to just do some gentle stretching or go for a walk in nature. After performing some gentle exercise you may want to do some meditation or visualization, such as progressive relaxation. You may spend some time in prayer or writing in your journal.

Finally, you may want to massage your body with a calming oil and then take a warm bath. Spend as much time as you want massaging and bathing yourself. Don't set up a rigid schedule to follow but intuitively partake in the various relaxing techniques described above that calm down your nervous system. You may want to spend the entire time during your mini retreat participating in just one activity.

I also recommend taking longer full-day or weekend retreats at least twice a year. You will feel rejuvenated after spending some time in a cabin in the woods or any place where you can have a few days of real peace.

Begin penciling in dates on your calendar for your nurturing mini retreats for this month. Once you have created specific times for your retreats, plan where you will have them. Before you begin your mini retreat, prepare a list of the items you will need to make the experience thoroughly relaxing.

You deserve to enjoy regular mini retreats, so enjoy many hours this week (and in the future) soothing your sensitive body, mind, and soul.

A Relaxing Drive

*M*ost HSPs experience stress when faced with time pressure at work or at home. Combined with your high sense of responsibility, functioning under time constraints can be one of the most difficult aspects of being a highly sensitive person. In the next five weeks you will practice specific techniques for dealing successfully with the daily pressures of our fast-paced modern society.

Try to avoid driving on the freeways during rush hour. If you must travel during a peak traffic hour, either use your city's mass transit system or, if it is practical, try to arrive at your destination earlier and spend the extra time taking a walk in nature or meditating.

Since HSPs are very conscientious, tardiness can create stress. It's important to leave early for your destination in case there are unexpected traffic jams. Worrying about being late to an appointment can really increase your anxiety level. I recently chose to cancel an appointment rather than sit in bumper-to-bumper traffic worrying about showing up late for the meeting. My cell phone came in handy that day.

It may be more relaxing to drive in the slow lane and let all the harried drivers pass you by. You may also want to listen to a calming tape or CD or classical music on the radio. Listening to pleasant music in the slow lane will help you transcend the stimuli-saturated world. But don't listen to a deep-relaxation tape or CD, since it can make you dangerously sleepy while driving.

Make a list of how driving creates tension in your life. Some examples are:

* Driving in traffic makes me feel anxious.

* I get upset easily when a driver cuts me off.

* I become upset when I'm late for work.

* Red lights drive me crazy when I'm in a hurry.

* I can't stand it when someone honks at me.

Now make a list of new coping strategies that you will employ this week when you drive. Some examples are:

* I'm going to take mass transit to work this week.

* I'm going to plan ahead so I don't get stuck in rush hour traffic.

* I'm not going to listen to talk radio this week when I drive.

✳ I'm planning on driving in the slow lane this week.

✳ I will look forward to a red light as an opportunity to do some slow abdominal breathing.

✳ I won't talk on my cell phone while driving.

When we are out of balance, we sometimes crave the things that will make us more out of balance. It may feel initially uncomfortable to turn off talk radio or drive slowly. However, the more you practice being in a peaceful state while driving, the more calm you will feel when you arrive at your destination.

Walking and Talking

Walking

In our fast-paced society, most people have become habituated to walking rapidly. One of the easiest and least expensive methods to reduce stimulation for the HSP is to take a walk in nature every day. Take this walk in silence—without conversation. While strolling in natural beauty, you may want to practice a walking meditation.

Try some of the following walking meditations this week:

*As you walk, try moving as slowly as possible and
become aware of your movements as you place one foot
leisurely in front of the other. Be aware as your heel and
toe touch the ground as you walk consciously.*

You may want to mentally repeat the mantra "peace" or "calm" with each step that you take. As you focus on your mantra, extraneous thoughts will no longer occupy your mind.

Another walking meditation is to simply take note of what you are hearing. Listen to the sweet songs of the birds, the flowing of a waterfall, or a squirrel scampering up a tree. Next, just observe what you are seeing. Gaze deeply at the cornucopia of multicolored flowers, the crystal-clear blue sky, or the velvety green grass. Next, become aware of what you are touching. Your shoes contact the soft ground and your arms gently stroke your coat as they sway back and forth. Spend some time enjoying these tactile sensations. Finally, just notice the activity of walking. Repeat in your mind "hearing, hearing," "seeing, seeing," "touching, touching," "walking, walking" as you do each action.

By practicing these walking meditations you will turn your walk in nature into a blissful experience. Initially you may want to copy these exercises and bring them with you on your walk. Walking meditation is an excellent way for the highly sensitive person to exercise the body while relaxing the mind.

Talking

Talking is an often overstimulating activity that HSPs have to constantly deal with. When you become involved in a rapid-fire discussion, it can be quite jarring to your sensitive nervous system. While most HSPs like to process information slowly, they are frequently pushed into a quick response by the majority non-HSP culture.

One of the most effective methods to reduce stimulation and create inner peace is to spend time in silence. When you are in silence in the presence of other people, you don't have to constantly give your opinion or defend yourself. You can just relax and simply observe people talking, which becomes a meditative experience. However, be aware of any rapid-fire thoughts that arise in your mind or your desire to give your opinion to boost your ego.

If you are a shy person, please don't use being in silence as an excuse to avoid interacting with people. We need to create a balance between our verbal interactions and quiet time.

It can be quite stressful for the HSP to respond quickly while conversing with others. A method that I have found very effective for reducing stimulation in intense conversations is the "pause for five seconds" technique. Both people agree to wait just five seconds before responding to the other person.

Try the following experiment today. Observe how you feel after talking rapidly. Are your muscles tense? Is your breathing shallow? Do you feel nervous? Next, spend some time talking very slowly and observe how your body and emotions feel.

Make a list of changes that you want to make this week in your verbal interactions. Some examples are:

✳ When I talk rapidly I will ask my family and friends to remind me to talk more slowly.

✳ I will spend some time each day in silence when I'm with other people.

✳ I will practice with my partner or with a friend the "pause for five seconds" technique.

At first it may feel uncomfortable to talk less, but as you begin to enjoy the peace and quiet of being in silence, you will want to choose your words carefully rather than saying the first thing that comes to mind.

Dining and Writing

Dining

We discussed in week 17 how the temperature and types of foods that you eat can adversely affect your nervous system. We will now discuss the importance of eating mindfully and slowly. Even if you eat only the healthiest organic vegetables, fruits, and whole grains, you still may get indigestion if you eat your meal too quickly.

The more mindfully you eat, the easier the food can be digested and the calmer you will feel. When you are aware of the food that you're eating, you will naturally feel more peaceful. Try to really taste the food during your meals this week. You may want to try eating in silence or with just minimal, light, pleasant conversation.

Mindful eating is a challenging practice to develop, especially for adults who were raised to eat while watching television or while always involved in intense conversations. Try focusing on the food that you're eating without engaging in any other stimulating activity (reading, watching television, surfing the Internet, talking, etc.). Try mindful eating for several meals this week. Mark these meals on your calendar and really savor the experience. Bon appétit!

Writing

Some HSPs feel pressured to write quickly, increasing their stress and tension. You may have a boss or instructor who demands that you complete written assignments quickly or you may have developed a habit of writing quickly from childhood. With the advent of the computer, most people don't do as much writing by hand. However, it is still beneficial to monitor your handwriting to reduce stimulation.

If you tend to write rapidly, you can learn to monitor your handwriting by trying the following exercise this week. After writing very quickly for a few minutes, close your eyes and see how you feel. Are you holding the pen or pencil tightly or are your hands tight? Is your breathing shallow or are your shoulders feeling tense?

Now consciously write very slowly and then be aware of how much more relaxed your body and mind feel.

If your handwriting is so poor that you can't read the last sentence you wrote, make yourself rewrite it slowly, enjoying the clear handwriting and a new sense of inner peace.

Telephoning

Cell Phones

With the increased use of cell phones (especially speaker cell phones), the stimulation in public venues can be overwhelming. Most HSPs find it extremely agitating to be forced to listen to other people's private discussions while shopping in a store, waiting in a bank line, or walking down the street. To deal with this bombardment of stimuli, you can listen to soothing music on your headset. You can change your seat if you are in a restaurant next to someone who is talking loudly on a cell phone. If someone is talking on a cell phone in a library or during a movie, you can ask them to please refrain from using their phone. I also recommend that you reduce tension by turning off your cell phone when you're driving. Some U.S.

post offices have signs that state that they will not wait on a customer who is talking on a cell phone. Hopefully other facilities will adopt this policy.

However, some positive aspects of owning a cell phone are that HSPs can receive instant support from others and feel more secure, especially in emergency situations.

List some ways that you can cope with cell phones this week. Some examples are:

* ✳ Plan to take a headset with you when you go out.

* ✳ Put on a headset or earplugs when people near you are talking loudly on cell phones.

* ✳ Move away from people talking into their cell phones if possible.

* ✳ Refrain from using a cell phone while driving.

* ✳ Politely ask people using cell phones in movie theaters and libraries to refrain from using them. You can also ask a clerk to ask the offender to stop using the cell phone if necessary.

By planning ahead, you won't become a casualty cell phone cacophony.

Oh No, Not Another Phone Call

Instead of hearing the ringing of your phone as another negative stimulus in your life, transform the sound into a relaxation cue. Just as if you were a member of a retreat being called to meditation with the sound of a bell, let the ringing be a reminder for you to practice deep relaxation.

Try the following experiment whenever the phone rings during this week. Try not to answer the phone until the third or fourth ring. Use those few moments to relax all your muscles while you take a few slow, deep breaths and mentally repeat a mantra such as "calm" or "peace." When you are feeling overwhelmed, instead of answering the phone with a curt, irritated hello, you'll answer the phone in a very slow, relaxed voice. Also, since HSPs tend to startle easily, it may be a good idea to lower the volume on your phone.

Answering the phone on the third or fourth ring is an easy practice to integrate into your life. Take time out now to write a small note to tape on your phone that reads: "Answer on the third or fourth ring; take slow, deep breaths." You will spend many precious moments today feeling peaceful by practicing deep relaxation when the phone rings.

Using the Computer

$\mathcal{T}$he overstimulating Internet and personal computer have become a foundation of life in the twenty-first century. Many people will have to spend much of their workday sitting in front of a computer. Try to take breaks every fifteen minutes for stretching or a short walking meditation. If this is not practical, you can simply close your eyes and watch your breath for a few moments. You should take regular breaks to avoid developing back, neck, and wrist pain. In addition to potential physical ailments, computer overuse can create eyestrain, nervousness, and a feeling of being overwhelmed as you are bombarded by stimuli.

What are some new strategies that you can employ this week to reduce overstimulation from computer usage? Some examples are:

✳ Take a computer fast one day a week.

✳ Limit nonessential time on the computer.

✳ Install a spam filter.

✳ Take a break every fifteen minutes for stretching and slow abdominal breathing.

✳ Reduce the number of e-mails that you send.

✳ Type at a slower rate.

✳ Set a timer in another room that will motivate you to leave your computer so that you will be able to stop and reflect on what you have been doing.

Spending an inordinate amount of time surfing the Internet is one of the most important factors that can create overstimulation for the HSP. It's essential for highly sensitive people to be discriminating regarding computer usage to maintain a sense of inner peace.

A Calming Diet for the HSP

$\mathscr{F}$or the next three weeks you will learn how diet affects highly sensitive people and learn techniques to implement a healthy diet. As an HSP it's important for you to be careful about your diet. Certain foods can actually increase tension and anxiety. Other foods may weaken your immune system.

Creating a Healthy Diet

Since you are constantly bombarded by advertisements that encourage you to buy unhealthy food, you need to get support from family and friends for developing new, healthy dietary habits. You may want to read books about the importance of a healthy diet and shop at health-food stores. It's best to avoid processed foods that may contain carcinogenic dyes, MSG (monosodium glutamate), excessive amounts of salt and sugar, and polyunsaturated fat. It's also good to avoid spicy foods, fast-food restaurants (which tend to sell food containing high levels of sugar, salt, fat, and chemicals), and the pesticides found on commercially grown fruits and vegetables.

Sometimes when your body is out of balance you may crave foods that throw you even more out of balance. For example, the more that you eat foods saturated with salt and sugar, the more you will tend to desire them. However, the more you eat calming, natural foods, the more you will crave the organic vegetables, fruits, and whole grains that will calm your nervous system.

When beginning a new diet it's best to incorporate the changes slowly. For example, you can reduce processed foods little by little as you add more organic vegetables, fruit, and whole grains into your diet.

It's also important not to overeat. If you leave half of the stomach empty, the body will digest the food properly, avoiding indigestion and tension. You may want to try fasting for just a few days if it's not cold outside. (When you fast, your body will tend to cool down since you're not ingesting food, which heats up the body.) However, it's generally not beneficial for the HSP to do long fasts, since your sensitivity may create adverse emotional and physiological reactions if you deprive yourself of food for many days.

Since every constitution is different, experiment to find the diet that can help you stay healthy. Which techniques to create a healthy diet do you want to try this week? Some examples are:

* ✳ I'm going to have a discussion with my family about our meals this week and explain to them why it's important that we make dietary changes.

* ✳ I will not snack after dinner tonight.

* ✳ This week I am only going to buy organic fruits and vegetables.

* ✳ I won't take the kids to a fast-food restaurant.

* ✳ When I do my grocery shopping, I will read the ingredients carefully.

* ✳ I'll reduce my consumption of processed foods.

* ✳ I will read some books and visit Web sites on healthy, natural recipes this week.

When you use discrimination about which foods you eat, your body will function at an optimal level.

A Sample Diet for the HSP

Calming Foods

According to Ayurveda, the healing system from India, eating foods that are heavy, warm, and moist can help promote calmness for the vata constitution, which tends to have a sensitive nervous system. Eating foods such as warm soup, casseroles, and hot cereal is both nurturing and calming, especially in the winter. I recommend eating more cooked vegetables in the winter and more salads in the summer.

Between meals you may want to eat a healthy snack such as fruit, veggies, nonfat yogurt, nuts, or seeds. Try a delicious snack that satisfies your sweet tooth by cutting up an apple and banana (or any fruit) and topping it with one tablespoon of natural (sugar-free) berry syrup or jam and shredded coconut. Try not to have sugary, processed foods in the house to avoid temptation, and stock your kitchen with healthy, natural foods.

Creating a Diet for the Week

Let's now create some sample menus that can help calm down your nervous system and maintain a healthy body. Since each HSP is unique, follow the diet that helps you feel calm and maintains your optimal health.

In *The Highly Sensitive Person's Survival Guide*, I recommended the following sample meals, which are particularly calming and healthy for the HSP.

Breakfast suggestions:

* ✳ Oatmeal or oat bran topped with nonfat plain yogurt, milk, or soymilk and fruit. You may also want to put some cinnamon on your cereal and use the herb stevia as a sweetener, which may help control blood sugar.

* ✳ Sprouted grain bread topped with salt-free butter, sugar-free jam, or soy or low-fat cheese.

* ✳ Eggs cooked in olive-oil cooking spray.

Lunch suggestions:

* ✳ A large portion of lightly steamed or lightly sautéed vegetables and/or salad with tuna, salmon, sardines, lean turkey, or chicken and sprouted bread. Top off

your cooked veggies with olive oil, low-salt soy sauce, or some nonfat yogurt, then garnish with sesame or sunflower seeds or nuts.

✳ Vegetable bean soup, cooked veggies, or salad with olive oil, and sprouted grain bread.

✳ Soy burger with lettuce and tomatoes on a sprouted grain bun with a large salad dressed with olive oil.

Dinner suggestions:

✳ A large portion of lightly steamed or lightly sautéed vegetables and/or salad dressed with olive oil, whole grains (brown rice, barley, etc.), broiled or baked fish, lean chicken or turkey.

✳ A low-fat casserole, served with cooked veggies or salad with olive oil.

✳ A hearty soup or stew, or your favorite healthy dish served with cooked veggies or salad dressed with olive oil.

Plan your meals for the week, making sure that you also make a list of ingredients and supplies that you will buy at the grocery store. Don't forget to purchase healthy snacks like fruit, veggies, nuts, seeds, and nonfat yogurt.

Be sure to choose foods that you enjoy in order to reinforce success in creating your new diet this week. Remember that the longer you stay on your new diet, the easier it becomes to follow.

Helpful Diet Hints

*W*hen cooking your vegetables, steam them for only two to three minutes so that they are still crunchy and have not lost their vitamins or enzymes. If you stir-fry your vegetables, you may want to use olive-oil cooking spray in a nonstick pan. Shop at your local health-food store and buy a huge selection of colorful organic veggies. Buy some new cookbooks on how to prepare healthy foods and keep them in an easily accessible place in your kitchen.

When eating a fattening main dish, try consuming only half of the normal serving, and eat the heavier foods very slowly, savoring the taste of each morsel. If you like fish, it's best to eat seafood that is high in omega 3 oils (such as salmon and sardines) and avoid fish that has high levels of mercury (such as shark, swordfish, and king mackerel). It's best to eat fruit between meals or two hours after eating a large meal since fruit does not digest well when combined with other foods.

Spend some time thinking about new approaches that you would like to try to help you prepare calming, nutritious meals. Write up these suggestions to incorporate into your cooking and dining this week and put the list in a prominent place in your kitchen. It's important to review your list of new approaches to your diet on a regular basis.

Exercise and Sports for the HSP

$\mathcal{I}$n the next three weeks you will learn how our culture has influenced your attitude toward exercise, which physical activities fit your sensitive temperament, and how to create a regular exercise program.

Your Participation in Physical Exercise

As an HSP, you'll want to engage in exercises that create inner peace. In order to avoid injury, it's vital that you exercise at a pace that is comfortable for your body. You should exercise at about 50 percent of your capacity, and you should be able to carry on a conversation or breathe through your nose. It's recommended that people engage in thirty minutes of moderate-intensity physical activity on most, if not all, days. However, these activities can be broken up into several shorter sessions that add up to thirty minutes during the day.

Our competitive sports culture is anathema for many HSPs and can be especially challenging for males. Many boys and girls are ostracized or teased if they are not adept in team sports at school. Playing group sports under pressure can create performance anxiety that can be overwhelming for the HSP, possibly creating poor self-esteem. More than 90 percent of the HSPs I surveyed reported that they prefer to participate in individual exercise rather than team sports. While some HSPs may be naturally athletic and, with practice, can cope with the pressure of team sports, individual and noncompetitive exercise is generally more in tune with the HSP temperament.

Write down a short history of your experiences with physical exercise and group sports from childhood to the present. Have there been any sports that have been physically and emotionally challenging for you? How did you deal with the situation? Have you shunned all exercise due to traumatic early experiences associated with sports? Please be gentle with yourself when writing this exercise since the assignment may bring up some unpleasant memories. If any emotional pain arises, just observe it and realize that you are so much more than any past painful experience.

In light of your new awareness about the relationship between highly sensitive people and the pressure of group sports, write down how your early childhood experiences in sports would have been different with supportive coaches, teachers, parents, and peers. Given the HSP's preference for individual physical activity, write down what activities would have been better for you to have participated in as a child in school.

Now it's time to give yourself a pat on the back for all the success you have had performing different exercises as an HSP. Write down all of your positive experiences performing physical activities. What activities have you enjoyed participating in?

As you investigate your connection with sports and physical activity in society, remember that we are living in an out-of-balance world that emphasizes competition, separation, and aggression at the expense of fun, cooperation, and compassion. If you or your HSP child wants to play team sports, choose a sport that is inherently less violent such as soccer or volleyball rather than American football or rugby. However, any player or coach with an insensitive attitude or a drive to win at all costs could turn any game into HSP hell. And conversely, any sport can be enjoyable if the consciousness of the participants is supportive and caring.

Physical Activities for the HSP

*A*s we discussed last week, it's best for HSPs to engage in noncompetitive physical activities. One of the easiest and least expensive exercises for healing your body and mind is to take a silent walk in nature every day. While walking, try to stay focused in the present moment by performing a walking meditation (as described in week 20). Meditating as you walk will help prevent you from identifying with negative thoughts that may arise, resulting in tension. If you enjoy competing in sports, it's probably best to play with just one other supportive person to reduce excessive stimulation and anxiety.

A method to exercise the body while reducing tension is hatha yoga, which originated in India but has become very popular in the West in recent years. Yoga postures consist of a series of stretching poses that tone the body while releasing stress. When you perform hatha yoga, you are exercising your body as well as calming your nervous system. Experienced yoga instructors will advise you to perform gentle movements and never to push yourself into a pose. Tai chi is another calming exercise, one that originated in China and is fast catching on in North America. Tai chi consists of slow and harmonious martial-arts movements that help promote a feeling of inner peace for the participant.

If you aren't currently exercising on a regular basis or feel tense after exercising, choose a new exercise to perform regularly beginning this week. Some examples are:

* Tai chi

* Walking

* Bike riding

* Swimming

* Using an exercise machine

* Yoga

* Cooperative games, like keeping a ball in the air

Every highly sensitive person is unique, so explore the type of exercise that works best for you. Make sure that you choose an activity that you really enjoy so that you will be motivated to exercise regularly.

An Exercise Schedule

$\mathcal{D}$uring exercise the body releases endorphins, which actually reduce stress. If you exercise with a family member or friend, your relationship will probably improve as you each enjoy the rush of positive endorphins creating a positive mutual experience. Always consult your physician before you begin an exercise program.

If you exercise at a health club, it's important to choose one that has a calming ambiance. An hour in a facility with loud, jarring music, bright fluorescent lights, and a crowd of noisy people could actually create more tension for the sensitive person. Try to exercise outside in a calm, natural environment as much as possible.

How can you create a regular exercise schedule this week? Some examples are:

✳ Exercise with a friend to create a support system.

✳ Exercise close to your home or office.

✳ Consider buying an exercise machine; place it in an area where you'll be likely to use it.

✳ Choose an exercise that you really enjoy.

✳ Don't push yourself to the point of exhaustion or strain.

✳ Work out at 50 percent of your maximum capacity.

Listen to interesting tapes or CDs on a headset player; watch an inspiring television show or movie or read while using an exercise machine.

Remember that regular aerobic exercise helps prevent heart disease, lowers blood pressure, helps you control weight, increases your energy and joy, and reduces stress and depression.

Alternative Medicine for the HSP

$\mathcal{G}$iven the HSP's proclivity to absorb stress that can create physical and emotional problems, it makes sense for us to use the effective supplements, vitamins, and herbal treatments that are available to help maintain our energy level, stay calm, and modify any adverse physiological reactions from stress. Many HSPs have told me that they are interested in taking supplements but feel overwhelmed and confused by the choices available, not knowing which to take.

In addition to the sheer number of supplements available, it can be hard to know where to turn for reliable information on supplements and herbs. Unfortunately, a situation has developed where millions of people are buying supplements and herbs, yet the American FDA (Food and Drug Administration) does not regulate the industry, and most medical doctors have not received any training in the subject.

While herbs and supplements are generally safe, you always have to be careful about side effects. If you are already taking allopathic medicine (conventional medicines prescribed by your doctor or bought over the counter), you need to be especially aware of the effects that vitamins and herbs may have on your body. For example, vitamin E can be dangerous to take with Coumadin, a blood thinner.

I strongly recommend that you consult with your physician before taking any herbs or supplements. If your doctor is not familiar with a supplement, you may want to meet with a holistic medical doctor. (To find a holistic medical doctor, please visit www.ahha.org, www.holisticmedicine.org, www .acam.org, or www.orthomed.org.)

There are many reputable medical doctors and medical researchers who have written books and articles describing the safe use of supplements and herbs for the public. There are also many holistic healers such as homeopaths, naturopaths, Ayurvedic practitioners, herbalists, and acupuncturists who are knowledgeable in prescribing supplements and herbs. However, it's important to make sure that your practitioner is really well informed on all of the side effects.

Your Medical Care

You may find that you're more comfortable with a holistic health-care practitioner because many of them are highly sensitive, while most medical doctors are not. It's important for you to let your doctor know that you are a highly sensitive person. Tell him or her that since you tend to feel things more deeply, your body could react to medication and pain more intensely than most people. This is important information for your doctor to know about you.

If your last physical exam was more than a year ago, call your doctor this week to schedule a thorough exam. Practice telling your doctor about your sensitivity on your next visit. (Please refer to week 5, "Informing Others About Your Trait.")

Would you like to consult with an alternative health-care provider? If so, this week set up an appointment with one of the following (please visit www.hspsurvival.com to find Web sites that list how to find alternative practitioners or read chapter 10 in *The Highly Sensitive Person's Survival Guide*):

* Acupuncturist

* Aromatherapist

* Ayurvedic practitioner

* Chiropractor

* Herbalist

* Holistic medical doctor

* Homeopath

* Hypnotherapist

* Massage therapist

* Naturopath

To cure what ails you and to improve your daily life, why not take advantage of all the options available to you: modern Western medicine, supplements and vitamins, and ancient healing herbs from indigenous cultures.

Buying Herbs, Vitamins, and Supplements

$\mathcal{T}$here are some excellent sources available offering information on herbs, vitamins, and supplements that we will review this week. Spend some time visiting the Web sites or reading the books of some of the following authors:

* Andrew Weil, MD, *Spontaneous Healing* (1995), www.drweil.com

* Deepak Chopra, MD, *Grow Younger, Live Longer* (2001), www.chopra.com

* Burton Goldberg, *Alternative Medicine: The Definitive Guide* (1993), www.burtongoldberg.com

* Jean Carper, *Stop Aging Now!* (1995), www.stopagingnow.com

Write down the information that you obtain from your research and implement a plan for beginning to use vitamins, herbs, and supplements this week. Be sure to consult with your doctor before taking new supplements.

It's important to check prices and quality of herbs and supplements before purchasing them. There are many discount health-food stores. However, because it's important to obtain the highest quality supplement from a reputable manufacturer, don't choose products just because they're cheap. You may want to talk with the buyer who orders vitamins and herbs at your local health-food nutrition store to determine which brand has a good reputation. Unfortunately, some stores hire people with little or no experience, so make sure the person you consult is well informed. If not, try another store.

Always ask the salesperson when the herb or supplement was manufactured, since the expiration date on the package may not be accurate. For example, flaxseed oil should be used within six months of the date of manufacture, yet sometimes the expiration date will be in one or two years. When taking herbs, unless you can be sure that the capsules (or loose herbs in a jar) are fresh, it is better to buy a tincture (liquid preserved in an alcohol or nonalcohol base). After six months some dry herbs begin to lose their potency, and in one year many herbs are not very effective. A tincture lasts up to five years.

Plan to visit your local health-food nutrition store this week. Some questions to explore during the visit may include:

* How long has the staff worked in the supplement department?

* Which supplement companies have the best reputation?

* Which supplements can help you with your specific physical and emotional challenges?

Write down the information you obtain at your health-food store and put it in your personal medical file.

Although the supplements, herbs, and vitamins may cost $50 or more a month, this preventative measure is still a fraction of the price that you may have to spend on allopathic medicine and doctor visits if you don't maintain a healthy body. An ounce of prevention is worth a pound of cure!

Herbs and Supplements to Calm the HSP

$\mathcal{T}$here are many herbs and supplements you can take to reduce anxiety and tension. However, it's generally not a good idea to take herbal preparations for stress reduction daily since your body may become habituated to the herb and could need larger dosages for the herb to be effective. Herbs for anxiety relief should be taken on an "as needed" basis.

Some commonly used herbs to reduce anxiety are valerian, passionflower, hops, and chamomile. Many HSPs have had good results buying a formula with a combination of calming herbs, which creates a synergistic effect. Everyone's system reacts differently to each herb as well as to the dosage. Ask your doctor or health care practitioner what dosage you should take. Since HSPs are more sensitive to the effects of herbs, you should begin with a small dose and slowly increase the amount you take under your health care provider's advice. Experiment with different herbs to see which one works best for your constitution. There are also three supplements that help calm the nervous system: taurine, glycine, and GABA. Finally, there is a marvelous flower essence tincture called "Rescue Remedy" that helps create calmness during stressful situations.

A great deal of the information in this book is based on the principles of the ancient healing system from India called Ayurveda. Some Ayurvedic herbs that calm the nervous system are jatamansi and ashwagandha. You may want to visit an Ayurvedic practitioner (visit www.hspsurvival.com for listings of Ayurvedic practitioners) or you can buy Ayurvedic herbs from Bazaar of India (www.bazaarofindia.com). Ayurvedic calming herbs in a sesame oil base are a potent relaxant that you may want to use when you're under stress (www.oilbath. com). You can apply the oil to your forehead and your ears to calm down the nervous system quickly as the soothing oil penetrates your skin.

Insomnia may occur when you travel or are under stress. You can take some calming herbs an hour before sleep. You may also want to try taking melatonin, which is the actual hormone that our brain releases when we go to sleep. You can take a time-released brand of melatonin an hour before bedtime to help you fall asleep or to minimize jet lag. If you're traveling by plane through many time zones, you may experience jet lag, making it difficult for you to fall asleep even if you're extremely tired. A homeopathic remedy called "No Jet Lag" can be helpful in reducing this effect.

Make a list and purchase any of the following herbs and supplements this week:

* Valerian, passionflower, or hops

* Chamomile

* A formula with a combination of anxiety-reducing herbs

* Taurine, glycine, and GABA

* Rescue Remedy

* Ayurvedic calming herbs such as jatamansi and ashwagandha

* The Ayurvedic calming oil prabhanjanam (www.oilbath.com)

* Melatonin

* No Jet Lag

Remember to consult with your doctor or qualified health practitioner before you begin taking vitamins, herbs, or supplements.

Creating Peaceful Relationships

$\mathcal{I}$n this section we are going to investigate how being a highly sensitive person influences relationships and learn techniques to create positive relationships with all beings.

As an HSP you may sometimes tend to overreact to other people's moods and behavior, often negatively. Highly sensitive children are deeply affected by their parents' painful emotional interactions with each other as well as toward them. These highly sensitive children from dysfunctional families tend to absorb their parents' pain like a sponge, setting themselves up for inharmonious relationships as adults.

Heart-Centered Meditation for the HSP

This week you will learn and implement some new methods to resolve conflicts with other people. Try the following exercises this week.

The following is called "The Heart-Centered Meditation" and is a simple exercise that can easily transform detrimental feelings of anger into love. By taping this visualization or having someone read it to you slowly, you will be able to go deeply into opening your heart and experience love.

Think of a recent experience when your reaction to being hurt by another person was to get angry. Is your attention focused in your head or heart?... Now breathe deeply and slowly into your belly... Focus on the air filling your abdomen and slowly exhale... Now shift your awareness to the left hand, left elbow, left shoulder, and left side of chest into your heart... Feel your heart expanding with love... Deeply experience the peace and harmony in the stillness and calmness of being centered in your heart... Next, visualize a positive experience that you've had with the same person... How did you feel toward that person then?... Take plenty of time to really visualize their good qualities... Ask yourself, can you let go of the anger?... Will you let go of the anger?... When will you let go of the anger?... The heart knows only love and will always let go of anger... Keep returning to the heart until you have released the anger... Once you have released the anger, you have shifted from a head-centered, judgmental framework to heart-centered, caring love.

Once-a-Week Mediation Program

One method of improving relationships that many HSPs have had success with is what I call the "Once-a-Week Mediation Program." Both people agree not to discuss contentious issues during the week. When people fight with each other on a daily basis, the relationship begins to deteriorate. Since the ego loves drama and conflict, you must become very alert not to identify with the negative thoughts arising in the mind toward a partner or with an intimate relationship. Unless the issue can be resolved immediately, both people should choose a specific time during the week to discuss the problem. Pick a time when you will both be relaxed and not under any time constraints; for example, on a weekend afternoon. During the week you may write down everything that disturbs you about the other person. By writing down your feelings and thoughts, you are not repressing your emotions or escalating the conflict by getting stuck in a daily verbal battle.

It's good for both people to meditate or do some slow, deep breathing before discussing a controversial subject. Begin the session by telling the other person the ways that you appreciate them. Both parties should agree to speak in a soft voice, since HSPs do not respond well to loud noises. During the mediation session, tell the other person how you feel rather than enumerating all the ways that the other person is wrong for doing things differently or having a different temperament. Try to see the situation from the other person's perspective by repeating back what they say and how they feel. Be open to compromise.

Try the Once-a-Week Mediation Program with your partner, family member, coworker, or with someone you are having trouble communicating with.

Conflict-Resolution Exercises

$\mathscr{T}$his week we are going to practice two more excellent techniques to reduce conflict in your life.

Pause for Five Seconds

In week 20, we discussed the "pause for five seconds" technique to reduce stimulation in conversation. Since HSPs tend to process information slowly, this technique is very helpful for keeping you centered. Both parties agree to pause for five seconds before responding to each other. You may want to remind the other person that HSPs need more time to process information. It's very difficult for a conflict to escalate when both parties agree to wait five seconds before responding. This process is a very effective tool for maintaining harmonious relationships for HSPs.

Who would you like to try the "pause for five seconds" technique with this week? It could be your partner, a family member, a friend, or someone at work.

The 1 Percent Apology

Another method that I have frequently recommended to assuage disagreements is called "The 1 Percent Apology." There are always two sides to any conflict. Take responsibility for your part in the argument, even if you believe it's only 1 percent of the problem, and simply apologize. Your expression of remorse gives an opening for the other person to apologize for their part in the disagreement—but don't expect or demand an apology. Even if the other person doesn't apologize, you have created peace of mind for yourself by opening your heart, not blaming anyone, and taking responsibility for your actions.

Is there someone with whom you've had a long-standing feud or recent conflict? When would you like to try The 1 Percent Apology technique with that person? Set a time for using this effective tool this week.

It would be beneficial to write down which conflict-resolution exercises worked best for you and continue utilizing those techniques on a regular basis.

Being in Silence

$\mathcal{S}$ince the highly sensitive person feels more peaceful in a quiet environment, it is important that we reduce the amount of time we spend talking. Being in silence with people lessens the potential for interpersonal conflicts. In addition, too much talking may deplete your energy level. It's important to choose your words carefully to avoid overstimulation.

Being in silence in a group setting can be very beneficial. You will feel more peaceful when you practice being quiet in large groups since you won't have to constantly state your opinions or talk about yourself. Self-centered talking can also inflate your ego, which tends to thrive on conflict, creating a vicious circle. If you are usually introverted in groups, this practice is not meant for you. Don't use silence as an excuse to avoid interpersonal connections, since the goal is to create a balanced life.

Is there a group event where you feel overwhelmed with the constant chatter? Inform the participants that you are going to be in silence during the activity.

Write down the dates and times of two group events where you will be in silence this week. Some examples are:

❋ A family function

❋ A meeting

❋ Spending an evening at home with the family in silence

❋ Nonessential talking at work

At first it may feel strange to be in silence with other people, but as you experience more joy during such quiet interludes, you will want to integrate this practice into more areas of your life. Make sure that you stay focused in the present moment rather than tuning out the conversation and worrying about the past or future. It may be a good idea to ask your family and friends to remind you to be in silence to reinforce this practice.

Stating What You Want

$\mathcal{S}$ince our aggressive society values non-HSP behavior, HSPs must learn how to create boundaries and speak up. Unfortunately, many HSPs are shy and feel embarrassed to state what they want. Since you may have been told throughout your life that there was something wrong with you for being sensitive, you may often suffer in silence or try to control the environment by withdrawing from difficult situations. However, if you repress your feelings, you can create frustration, isolation, and depression. When you practice asserting yourself from a loving place, you can make positive changes in all your relationships.

It's helpful to make a personal connection with someone before you request that they change their behavior. In some situations it is useful to state that you have a finely tuned nervous system before you request that the person change their behavior. This would be a good time to practice what you memorized in week 5 about informing others about your trait.

Is there a person in your life with whom you are experiencing challenges due to your sensitivity? Write down and practice how you can assert yourself in a positive manner using the following points:

1. Make a personal connection with the person, such as asking them about their work, family, hobbies, or vacation plans.

2. Let the person know (or remind them) that your nervous system is especially sensitive.

3. Tell the person that they are not doing anything wrong and take responsibility for your finely tuned nervous system.

4. Make your request in a kind manner. Brainstorm possible compromises with the other person, asking which possible solutions could work for them.

5. Thank the person for their consideration and ask them if there is anything that you could do to help them.

Heart-Centered Assertion

To enhance your ability to speak up, you may want to take an assertiveness-training class, discuss the situation with a counselor, or role-play the scenario with a friend. Try the following guided visualization before asserting what you want:

Breathe slowly and deeply into your belly for a few moments… Focus your attention on your heart… Visualize telling the offending person from your heart what you want… Notice that the person is unaware of how their behavior is affecting you… If this is someone you have a relationship with, imagine telling the person that you have a finely tuned nervous system… Then envision politely asking the person to change their behavior… Now clearly observe the person making the positive change…

When we assert ourselves from a loving and nonjudgmental place, there is an excellent probability that we will make positive changes in our life. The other person may be unaware that their behavior is irritating you. If you wait too long before stating your needs, you will tend to overreact when you finally ask them to stop their annoying habit.

Write down the name of the person and date that you will assert yourself in a kind manner. If you don't feel comfortable speaking to the person directly, you can always write a letter or send an e-mail. However, do not write to the other person when you are emotionally upset. Practice the heart-centered visualization first.

Sometimes you may deal with less accommodating people who may resent your asking them to make any changes in their life. You may need to come up with some creative solutions.

Sometimes it's more prudent to surrender to minor temporary inconveniences than to assert yourself. If the person reacts in a hostile manner, you may have to make changes in your lifestyle. Remember that your goal in life is peace of mind, not to give others a piece of your mind.

Once you increase your self-esteem and feel more peaceful, you'll lessen any temptation to bring belligerent people into your life and will attract more loving people. You will feel more peaceful simply by becoming aware of any tendency to create drama in your relationships. Therefore, one of the most important factors that determines harmony in relationships is your focusing on being in an inner state of peace.

Sharing Spiritual Experiences

$\mathcal{I}$n the next three weeks you will learn methods to spiritualize your relationships. Your interactions with others can become more harmonious when you create a spiritual connection with others.

Instead of wasting precious moments arguing about sensitivity differences, consider new activities that are fun and inspiring for all concerned. Take a spiritually uplifting walk in nature with your partner, family, and/or friends. You may also want to spend some time each day performing regular spiritual practices with your family and friends. When you have spiritual practices that you can do with those you love, the soul connection grows stronger, making it easier to transcend petty differences in temperament.

What are some spiritual activities that you can engage in with your family and friends this week? Some examples are:

* Taking a relaxing walk in a park or woods

* Spending an afternoon by a lake, a river, or the ocean

* Watching the sunrise or sunset

* Meditating

* Praying

* Reading a spiritual book together

* Watching a spiritually inspiring movie

People who engage in enjoyable activities together have less frequent arguments. Since HSPs thrive in calm, natural environments, it's quite relaxing to arrange outings to the ocean, rivers, mountains, or forests. However, when HSPs are involved in overstimulating activities like eating out in large, noisy restaurants, the spiritual connection can be stifled. It's important to compromise with your non-HSP family members and friends when planning activities. While it's all right to occasionally push yourself to be in stimulating environments for small periods of time, try not to go beyond your threshold to placate your non-HSP family and friends.

Make a list of activities that you engage in with your family and friends. Rank them according to what you consider the most to least stimulating. This list will help you create more relaxing events when you want to compromise with your non-HSP friends and family during the week and in the future. A sample list may include:

✳ Attending a large professional sporting event

✳ Going to a just-released, popular movie on a Saturday night

✳ Going shopping at a mall on a weekday

✳ Going to a lecture

✳ Dining at a quiet restaurant before the dinner rush on a weekday night

✳ Inviting a few friends to dinner

✳ Going with just the family or one friend on a relaxing walk in nature

✳ Gardening with a family member or friend

Keep your list of activities in a prominent place so that you can easily decide how much stimulation you can deal with before making plans.

Healing Meditations

*W*hen you relate to another on a soul level instead of on a transitory personality level, your relationships will improve. When you nurture the divine qualities in other people by spreading kindness, the light of higher consciousness will bloom in all your relationships.

It's important to feel compassion for less sensitive people. You don't want to become an "insensitive" sensitive person. While the non-HSP tolerance may be higher for loud noises, strong smells, and bright lights, non-HSPs also can experience tension when they are overstimulated.

Sending Love and Light Meditation

Choose someone who has mistreated you either in the past or present. The following is an effective visualization to perform this week to heal the hurt and let go of anger.

Sit in a comfortable position and close your eyes. Inhale slowly through your nose into your abdomen to the count of five… Hold to the count of five … and slowly exhale to the count of five. Feel your body becoming more and more relaxed with each exhalation.

Spend a few moments thinking about someone who has mistreated you. Now focus your energy in your heart and meditate on how that person is longing for love and approval. Spend some time sending them loving, healing white light. Visualize the healing energy transcending their outer shell and entering into their heart. Observe a seed of divine love being planted in their heart. Feel the person softening and opening to divine love as you continue to send them healing energy.

The more that you practice forgiving and feeling a sense of unity toward others, the more your positive spiritual connection with everyone increases. If you accidentally poke your eye with your finger, you will comfort both your finger and your eye. You won't blame your finger. Likewise, when you experience your divine connection with all sentient beings, you will want to always help others as you would yourself.

Unity with All Sentient Beings Meditation

To complete the following visualization, you can have someone read the meditation, or you may want to record it and play it back. This is an excellent spiritual activity to share with your family and friends this week.

Close your eyes and breathe deeply and slowly, focusing on your belly rising and falling. Feel all the muscles in your body relax from head to toe. Visualize yourself sitting in a room.

Feel your energy expanding from your heart. If there are other people in the room, feel your unity with them. Now clearly see the home or building that you are sitting in as your energy opens further to include any other beings, including pets and plants, in the structure... Your energy is now expanding further to include everyone in your neighborhood ... your town... Now your energy is enlarging so that you feel your unity with all sentient beings in the entire state... Your energy is getting so big that you include all souls in your country... Your inner light knows no boundaries as the light connects you with all of humanity and all the creatures and plants on the entire planet... The light makes a quantum leap, and you are now one with all beings in all the galaxies of the universe.

(long pause) When you're ready, feel your inner light returning to the Earth plane ... your country ...

your state ... your city ... your neighborhood ... this
building ... and finally back into the room.

This is a helpful visualization to practice when you're feeling that you are different for being a highly sensitive person.

Helping Others Brings You Joy

*O*ne of the most important aspects of being an HSP is your ability to feel compassion for suffering humanity. Obsessing about how someone has hurt your feelings only makes the situation worse. You can transform these lingering negative feelings by showing acts of kindness and compassion toward others. If you perform acts of kindness, you will be using your innate sensitivity to heal yourself as well as the world.

When you dwell on interpersonal problems, you may feel depressed; but when you perform kind deeds by helping others, the endorphins that are released in your body will literally make you feel joyful. In addition, you will transcend the self-centered ego that focuses on problems and experience divine joy in the present moment.

Make a list of some acts of kindness that you would like to do. Try to do several random acts of kindness each day this week. Some examples are:

* Make a meal for an elderly neighbor.

* Volunteer to help at a homeless shelter.

* Play a game with a lonely child.

* Visit patients in a nursing home.

* Do your partner or housemate's chores.

* Say a kind word to the harried salesclerk.

* Let the driver in the other car go in front of you.

* Genuinely compliment your family, friends, and coworkers.

It's virtually impossible to spend time thinking about how someone has hurt your feelings in the past or worrying about the future when you're focused in the present moment, serving humanity. Be sure to notice how good it makes you feel when you are partaking in those activities.

Releasing Stress at Work

$\mathcal{D}$uring the next five weeks you will learn how to reduce stress at work while creating a relaxed job environment. It is challenging for sensitive people to work under time pressure, for an inconsiderate boss, or with difficult colleagues. Over 95 percent of the HSPs that I surveyed stated that stress at work affects their physical or emotional health.

Due to your conscientiousness and desire to fulfill your obligations at work, you may find yourself frantically multi-tasking, trying to complete arduous assignments, resulting in emotional and physical burnout. Even in less overwhelming situations, your desire to be conscientious and not make mistakes can create stress. The feeling of not being able to live up to the non-HSP type A work standards can create frustration, anxiety, and low self-esteem for the HSP.

Depersonalization at work is a major cause of both stress and unhappiness on the job. The lack of human contact at work contributes to a feeling of anomie in the workplace.

Some stressful job conditions can be ameliorated if you work with a supportive staff. When you are performing work that you feel is meaningful, your job satisfaction increases. For example, if you can understand how your job is benefiting humanity, you will likely become more enthusiastic about your vocation.

Make a list of the areas that cause you stress at work. Some examples are:

❋ My boss pressures me to finish difficult assignments too quickly.

❋ I don't get any support at work.

❋ Some of my coworkers are rude.

❋ I am bored with my work routine.

❋ I'm only working at my job for the money.

❋ I'm frequently asked to work overtime.

When you can specifically identify the causes for tension at work, you will be able to make the necessary changes to create a more peaceful work environment.

When you use your willpower to decide that you will be happy at work, the probability that you will enjoy your job will improve. For example, when you set the intention to improve your relationships with people at work, your job satisfaction will increase. However, if you put forth a great deal of energy to improve a difficult job situation and nothing works, you can always quit. You are never stuck.

Creating a Calm Work Environment

$\mathcal{T}$his week we are going to discuss many specific methods to help create a more peaceful work environment for you. You can develop a daily work schedule to reduce stimulation rather than immediately jumping into a busy workday every morning. When you first arrive at work, center yourself by spending a few moments either meditating or doing some slow, deep abdominal breathing. Look at your assignments for the day and decide, given your sensitivity, what is a realistic expectation of tasks you can complete.

Try to do progressive relaxation for a few moments every hour by visualizing all the muscles in your body relaxing further and further as you take some slow, deep breaths. You may also want to meditate for short periods of time during your lunch hour or during breaks. Investigate with your supervisor the possibility of creating a meditation room at work. You could point out that employees' efficiency would improve if they had a peaceful room to meditate in for short breaks during the day. A quiet, dark room is a godsend for the HSP who works in a stimulating environment.

HSPs with insomnia usually find it stressful to be at work early every morning. Ask your employer about the possibility of arriving at work later in exchange for taking a shorter lunch hour or working a little later in the day.

If you enjoy going to work early, it can be beneficial for HSPs to start the day in a peaceful manner with few distractions. You can explore with your boss if you could do some work from home, which is ideal for the HSP.

Consider which of the examples below are germane to your workplace and incorporate some of the suggestions into your work this week. Some examples are:

* Listen to calming background music with a headset.

* Put up inspiring pictures of natural settings such as land- or seascapes.

* Bring flowers and plants to your office.

* Use aromatherapy at work, if possible.

* Surround yourself with love by putting up pictures of family and friends.

* Have a comfortable chair to sit in throughout the workday.

✻ Answer the phone on the third or fourth ring; use the time to do some deep breathing.

✻ Create a daily work schedule.

✻ Try to work in a slower and more focused manner.

✻ If you're sitting all day at work, take walking or stretching breaks.

✻ Do progressive relaxation or meditation.

✻ Have some uplifting magazines available to create a peaceful environment.

✻ Have calming herb tea and healthy snacks, like fruit, available.

✻ Recommend that your supervisor install a suggestion box.

✻ Change your work hours, if possible, or work from your home.

✻ Keep your sense of humor and smile frequently.

If you are feeling anxious at work, the tension amongst your colleagues will grow. However, when you implement relaxation techniques this week to create inner peace, your coworkers will also become calmer.

Resolving Conflicts with People at Work

$\mathcal{M}$any HSPs have told me how difficult it is for them to deal with rude and noisy people at work. In *The Highly Sensitive Person's Survival Guide*, I described how a student of mine resolved her challenges with a disruptive coworker. Monica, a single woman in her early thirties who worked for a state agency, reported that noise at work distracted her to the point that she couldn't concentrate on her duties. She worked in a small office with another woman who talked incessantly on the phone, complaining about her personal problems to friends in a loud, abrasive voice. Monica dreaded going to work in the morning and left her job with a tension headache almost daily. Although Monica was furious, she was afraid that if she asked the coworker to be quiet, the strained relationship would worsen.

We explored many options available to Monica to improve her intolerable work situation. For instance, she could wear a headset or earplugs, change the location of her desk, discuss the problem with her supervisor, or transfer to another department. I reminded her that the coworker might not even be aware that her talking was disturbing Monica. However, the colleague could probably subtly pick up Monica's anger, which could make a resolution more difficult. I suggested that Monica befriend the coworker (HSPs often escalate the problem by labeling a noisy person the enemy).

I then told Monica that once she developed a good rapport with her colleague, she could tell her (or write her a note) that she has a very sensitive nervous system, which makes normal noise sound amplified. Monica needed to emphasize that it is *her* problem and not blame the coworker. She could then offer several options to the colleague to resolve the difficulty, such as suggesting that the woman talk about personal issues during a certain agreed-upon time. During those intervals, Monica would be prepared and could take a break, go to lunch, or focus on work that could be done wearing a headset.

She could also politely ask if the coworker could speak in a lower voice or use another phone for personal calls. Finally, Monica should apologize in advance for any problems that her sensitivity might cause the coworker and tell her how much she appreciates the colleague's willingness to help her. The truth is that if Monica were a non-HSP, the coworker probably would not have to make any changes since many non-HSPs can tolerate or not even notice annoying sounds. If the colleague was amenable to any of the suggestions, Monica could bring her some flowers with a thank-you note to reinforce her appreciation for the coworker's assistance. After thinking about the issue for a few weeks, Monica finally wrote a note to her coworker and worked out a compromise that the colleague would make personal phone calls only during her lunch hour.

Is there a coworker at your job who is challenging for you? If so, try this exercise.

1. Using Monica's story as a blueprint, write down how you intend to negotiate with this colleague to resolve the situation. Are there any new options that you can implement to reduce the tension?

2. You may want to role-play what you will tell the coworker before the actual interaction. Make a specific date to deal with the situation this week.

3. How can you develop a good rapport with the person? Is there something about their life or interests that you can discuss?

4. Next, write down how you will explain your HSP trait. You may want to refer to what you wrote down in week 5 about informing others about your trait.

5. When you begin discussing solutions, emphasize that the coworker is not doing anything wrong. Apologize in advance for any difficulties your sensitivity is causing them and express appreciation for their kindness in

accommodating you. Explore various options with the colleague, asking if they would be willing to consider any of them.

6. To reinforce the colleague's new behavior, what can you do to show your appreciation?

If you assume that the other person is so belligerent that they would never change, you will create a negative self-fulfilling prophecy. However, if you approach the coworker from a positive, loving space, the probability is high that the difficult work situation will be resolved.

Earning More Money Can Create More Stress

$\mathcal{I}$t will increase your sense of well-being to work in a less demanding job that may pay a lower salary but give you the freedom to spend more time pursuing enjoyable and calming activities. Materialistic cravings create a vicious cycle. The more money people make, the more money they think they need. The more ego gratification employees receive on the job, the more status they will crave. If you make your job your entire life, you are setting yourself up for emotional trauma when you eventually leave the job or retire. It's better to live a balanced life, making time for a satisfying social life and pursuing interesting activities outside of work.

Are you either working too many hours or enduring severe job pressure just for the money? If so, list ways that you can make changes in your life so that you won't feel that you need to earn so much money. Some examples are:

✳ I'll consider relocating to an area where housing is cheaper.

✳ I don't really need such a big house.

✳ I can stay at a cabin in the woods during my vacation instead of going to an expensive, overstimulating resort.

✳ This week I'll meet with a vocational counselor to investigate other job possibilities that are more in tune with my HSP temperament.

✳ I will meet with a financial advisor to investigate ways to live more cheaply.

✳ Since my car is running well, I'll postpone buying a new car.

✳ I'll meet with a counselor to investigate why I need to sacrifice my happiness for material gain.

In our materialistic society, even HSPs may adopt the belief that making more money—even at the cost of your physical, emotional, and spiritual well-being—is worth it. Once your basic needs have been met, you may sometimes still drive yourself to earn more and more money, falsely believing that external remuneration will bring inner happiness.

Creating a New, Stress-Free Job

$\mathscr{C}$lients frequently tell me that they are dissatisfied with their job and want to explore a new field. I always advise them to be practical when pursuing new vocational goals. If you work in a job that pays well, it may not be beneficial to abruptly quit.

If you are interested in investigating a new, stress-free job, please follow these steps this week. First, make a list of your transferable skills and analyze how your skills apply to other vocations. What related vocations utilize your skills? For example, if you are an administrative assistant at a hotel, some of your transferable skills may include:

* Knowledge and expertise of specific computer programs

* Good public relations skills

❋ Expertise in bookkeeping and accounting

❋ Knowledge of the hospitality industry

❋ Experience in booking large events

❋ Knowledge of catering

Next, determine if your transferable skills match those mentioned in various job descriptions. You can look on the Internet or in newspapers for job qualifications or peruse *O*NET Dictionary of Occupational Titles* (Department of Labor 2004) at your local library.

The next step is to volunteer in the vocation that you would like to pursue. Volunteering is an excellent way to obtain experience that could lead to a paid job in the future. Another option is to begin working part-time in a new job that could possibly turn into a lucrative full-time position.

❋ Check the Internet and newspapers, network with friends, call your local volunteer bureau, or visit facilities to find a place to volunteer or work part-time.

❋ Make sure that your volunteer or part-time job does not interfere with your ability to continue working in your present position.

Before venturing into a new line of work, perform a labor market survey by doing the following:

❋ Contact at least ten people who work in the field that you want to go into. Ask about current hiring levels,

salary, and qualifications as well as the physical and
emotional demands of the job.

✳ Spend some time observing the new work environment. As an HSP, it's important to realistically eval-
uate if the job is suitable for a sensitive person. Pay
close attention to the stimulation level, job pressure,
and work hours. (Since HSPs generally process information slowly, take plenty of time to perform the labor
market survey. Don't become overwhelmed with too
much data or rush to make a quick decision.)

Investigate the following areas to get information about
the appropriateness of new job possibilities for HSPs:

✳ Read Elaine Aron's informative chapter on thriving at
work in her book *The Highly Sensitive Person* (1996).

✳ Read Barrie Jaeger's book, *Making Work Work for the
Highly Sensitive Person* (2004).

✳ Meet with a vocational counselor to discuss your
employment needs as an HSP.

✳ Take vocational tests to determine your interests,
abilities, and aptitude for various professions.

Self-employment can be an excellent option for HSPs who
don't want to work under the pressure of a boss and wish to
control the hours and level of stimulation. However, you need
to be willing to make difficult decisions and be careful not to
isolate yourself too much. If you work alone, it's important to

meet with colleagues regularly for support. Introverted HSPs could also have some challenges with the marketing aspect of self-employment. It's important to choose a field where you won't need to be working 24/7.

Before beginning self-employment, it's important to complete a thorough investigation as to the feasibility of success for your new vocational goal by meeting with a vocational specialist who helps people start their own businesses.

A Spiritual Life Calms the HSP

$\mathcal{O}$ne of the best attributes of being an HSP is your inherent capacity to have deep spiritual experiences. In this final section of the book, we are going to discuss ways to develop your spiritual connection with the divine, which will bring you inner peace.

The more you develop your sense of spirituality, the easier it will be to cope with daily overstimulation. Some of us may have a resistance to pursuing a spiritual path due to early negative religious experiences. You may want to think of spirituality in terms of unconditional love, beauty in nature, or a Higher Power. You may also be more comfortable relating spiritually to a specific deity or teacher like Christ, Buddha, or Krishna, or to a prophet like Abraham, Mohammed, or Moses. I know one person who is an agnostic but acknowledges that there is a mystery to life when he considers the vastness and the order of the universe.

Transcendence Through Spiritual Practices

Essentially all religions teach the same thing—to love the divine Higher Power and to be compassionate to others and yourself. The more we can take comfort in the divine presence within, the better able we will be to cope with life's challenges. The stable, unwavering love of God gives us succor during stressful times.

Spend some time thinking about your spiritual orientation as an HSP. Write down some examples of how your attunement to the divine has helped you during challenging times. How can your spiritual practices help you with a current challenge? Some examples are:

✳ Whenever I feel the peace of God in nature, watching a beautiful sunset, or looking at the vastness of the universe on a clear starry night, my job worries become insignificant.

✳ Instead of being upset about my divorce, I close my eyes and focus on my inner body, feeling divine energy flowing through me until I become peaceful.

✳ When I get angry at my partner, I inwardly ask, "Who is getting angry?" When I realize that it's the temporarily hurt ego that's upset and that I'm so much more than just the angry thoughts arising in my mind, I'm able to release the anger.

✻ I pray deeply for my mother's health to improve and then after I experience a profound divine connection, I feel that God's will is done regardless of the outcome.

✻ Whenever I accept a challenging situation in the present moment instead of wishing that things were different, I know that everything happens in divine right order.

The Limits of the Human Ego

*O*nce you understand the nature of people, you will probably gain more serenity in your life. Almost no one loves another more than their own self, and virtually everyone's motivation is based on self-interest. When you let go of attachment to the notion that people should act in a certain way, you can experience more inner peace. Therefore, by understanding the nature of the world, you will be able to act from your inner essence rather than constantly overreacting to the moods of people and ever-changing situations.

Many people will treat you nicely because they want something from you. Notice how polite salespeople are when they want you to buy their product. Frequently, the person who said they would love you forever leaves when you don't give them what they want. The nature of a human being's egotistical love is conditional. However, divine love, as exemplified by the true saints such as Christ, Buddha, or Mother Teresa, is unconditional.

Spend some time thinking about a situation where you were helpful to another person and felt hurt that the other didn't reciprocate. Ask yourself if you were behaving in a caring manner because you wanted something from the person. Then spend some time meditating on the truth that if you were truly giving from a place of unconditional love, you wouldn't expect anything in return.

Given your new understanding that almost no one loves another more than their own self, and virtually everyone's motivation is based on self-interest, revisit the situation where you felt hurt by another person's behavior. Do you still feel as hurt knowing that this is the nature of human behavior?

Now write down how you feel about the same situation in view of your new understanding.

As you begin to understand the nature of the human ego, which is based on self-interest, you won't be so disappointed when you realize that some egotistical people are simply not capable of treating others in a compassionate manner.

Remembering Your True Spiritual Nature

As a sensitive soul, you may find it easy to get bogged down in the little discomforts of life and forget that what seems so important today will hardly matter next month or next year. Once you deeply understand that your soul's brief journey in this incarnation will pass by swiftly, you won't get caught up in the false belief that you are only this sensitive body.

While our family, home, and bank account will all disappear when we leave our body, the love that we've shared and our spiritual attunement to the divine will last eternally. When we die, our souls will not be black or white, Muslim or Christian, male or female, sensitive or insensitive. When we experience the flow of divine energy connecting all beings, our fleeting differences hidden behind the masks of temporary personalities will become less important.

Spend a few minutes with your eyes closed, relaxing all the muscles in your body. Take a few slow, deep breaths. Focus on a time when you experienced a deep spiritual transformation. Spend as much time as you need remembering the uplifting experience. Where were you when the experience happened? Remember how the sensations in your body felt at that time. Did you notice any special colors or hear any beautiful sounds? How did it feel to go beyond daily body consciousness? Now write down the spiritual experience in as much detail as you can remember.

It will be beneficial to read about your spiritual experience during your morning or evening routine or when you are involved in an emotionally challenging situation.

Viewing Your Soul from an Eastern Perspective

Another way to explore your true spiritual nature is from an Eastern philosophical perspective based in Buddhism or Hinduism. From that perspective, any suffering that people experience in life is due to negative karma acquired from this life or previous incarnations. All the positive events in life are based on the merits one has gained in this or in previous lives. Looking at your situation from that viewpoint, you might consider that perhaps you were an insensitive person in a previous life and now you must experience a sensitive nervous system in this life. From a Western, Judeo-Christian perspective, many HSPs have also felt more peaceful realizing that they will reap the results of their actions. We can always lessen the effects of our karma during challenging times by performing good deeds, prayer, and meditation and focusing on the present moment.

Spend a few minutes with your eyes closed, relaxing all the muscles in your body. Take a few slow, deep breaths. Consider your sensitive nervous system from either the Eastern philosophic belief of karma or the Western viewpoint of reaping the results of your actions. Do you feel some comfort realizing that on a soul level, you are supposed to be a highly sensitive person in this lifetime? Does it help you feel that you are not a victim? Is it easier for you now to go forward with a more positive attitude toward life?

Write down what this contemplation was like for you in as much detail as possible. It will be beneficial to refer to this passage during your morning and evening routine.

While sometimes we may despair that our sensitivity is creating many challenges in life, the perceived obstacles can be opportunities for us to grow closer to God.

Watching Your Thoughts

*W*hile it is difficult for sensitive people to remain detached during stressful situations, the more you practice observing life's challenges, the less minor disturbances will irritate you. Identification with negative thoughts will only perpetuate problems.

If you can step back and just observe thoughts and emotions rather than immediately reacting and identifying with them, you will develop the spiritual quality of detachment. When you find yourself obsessing about how, for example, someone hurt you, simply step back and watch the thought. Just note how the ego/mind continues feeding the conflict, resulting in emotional pain and strife for you as well as the other person. As you remove yourself from being an active participant in the conflict in your mind, ask yourself what the next thought will be. When that thought has arisen, just inquire what the next thought will be. As you begin to observe the thoughts floating by without attaching to them, you will begin to realize that you are more than the myriad of negative thoughts racing through your mind.

At the moment you become aware that emotional pain from the past wants to renew itself through more negative thinking, you enter the present moment and the emotional pain dissolves. When you find yourself acting like a victim, obsessing on how you have been hurt, simply become aware that these thoughts are not you, but only the hurt inner child within you who is trying to perpetuate the false role of one who suffers. As you become aware of the negative thoughts, you will cease to identify with them. The false belief that you must suffer like a helpless child then dissipates, since emotional pain cannot survive in the present moment in a state of awareness.

Which of the following spiritual practices would you like to begin this week in order to develop detachment? Some examples are:

* Observing your thoughts as they arise in meditation

* Practicing awareness of how the ego wants to create separation and pain

* Feeling divine energy flowing through your body

* Throughout the day, simply observing sights and sounds in the present moment

* Practicing a walking meditation

✳ Repeating a mantra

✳ Reading spiritual books about how to release negative thinking, such as *A New Earth* by Eckhart Tolle (www .eckharttolle.com) or *Loving What Is* by Byron Katie (www.thework.com)

The more you can just watch the drama of life unfold around you as if you were in a movie theater, gazing at the ever-changing shadows of darkness and light, the more your tranquility will increase.

Seeing the Good in Others

$\mathcal{S}$ometimes HSPs tend to focus on the little irritations caused by other people. However, the more you concentrate on the positive characteristics of others, the happier you will become. Use your inherent deep compassion to forgive everyone and open your heart through acts of loving kindness. Complaining about other people only creates a downward spiraling of energy that can weaken your immune system and may even create physical or emotional illness.

Ask a friend or family member to remind you not to make any negative remarks about people this week and in the future. Or, set a timer to ring hourly throughout the week to remind you to be aware of any judgmental thoughts or statements about other people.

Although you may experience negative emotions such as fear, anger, hatred, and jealousy more strongly than others, you also can feel love more deeply than most non-HSPs. Since love is the strongest emotion, you can use its power to heal your relationships, if you choose to.

Equipped with your infinite capacity to express compassion, you too can overcome hatred with love as you dive deeply to discover the positive characteristics hidden in even the most insensitive person.

Make two genuine, heartfelt statements of appreciation every day this week. You may want to begin by appreciating your family and friends. Expand your gratitude to include strangers such as salesclerks or other customers in a store. Finally, find something to appreciate about insensitive people you encounter.

Make a list of the people whom you have appreciated this week and what you said. How can you continue this practice in the future?

Notice how spiritually uplifted both you and the other person feel after you have made genuine statements of appreciation. Everyone wants to feel loved and approved of, and by expressing positive energy you've created a little more love on the planet for others as well as yourself.

Centering Yourself

𝒯he effectiveness of acupuncture demonstrates that there are flows of energy throughout the body that need to be open so that energy isn't blocked. There are seven energy centers (or chakras) in the human body, and HSPs may tend to have their higher energy centers open, while the lower ones may be closed. When highly sensitive people live solely from the upper four energy centers of the crown (top of the head), the third eye (the point between the eyebrows), the throat region, and the heart, they are more prone to absorb other people's energy. When the lower energy centers in the area of the abdomen, base of the spine, and the area slightly below the base of the spine are closed, the HSP may not be grounded.

By opening the lower energy centers, the HSP will become more centered, allowing for a flow of energy throughout the body. This balanced energy flow will help you better cope with stimuli. The centering meditation described in week 8 is especially helpful for becoming grounded. You may also want to put heavy (grounding) oils such as sesame oil on your lower energy centers or eat cooked root vegetables, which also can help you feel centered.

What can you do to remain more centered this week? Some examples are:

* Practicing the centering meditation

* Balancing your energy centers by feeling the energy flowing through each of your chakras

* Making an appointment with a Reiki or acupuncture practitioner

* Eating heavy, cooked foods

* Taking regular meditation breaks

* Performing slow, deep abdominal breathing

* Gardening

The more centered we become, the less we will be affected by the ups and downs of life.

The Benefits of Meditation

$\mathcal{M}$any spiritual teachers have taught that the purpose of being born human is for the individual soul to expand into God's infinite love and light. Through meditation, highly sensitive people can easily experience the divine effulgent energy flowing through us. Throughout this book we have discussed the benefits of meditation. Through inner contemplation and reflection, you can develop your innate spiritual ability and calm your nervous system. I have observed many of my HSP students experiencing a phenomenal spiritual transformation as I led them in guided meditation. They may come to class feeling agitated, but after even a short meditation, the HSP easily enters into a calm and blissful state.

While noise or intrusive thoughts may distract you during meditation, you can still receive many benefits by integrating this practice into your daily life. You never know when you will be blessed with a profound spiritual experience. Many HSPs have reported suddenly experiencing feelings of bliss even during a restless meditation.

Sit quietly for a few minutes and contemplate how even a short meditation will help you feel calmer as you transcend your daily outer problems and experience the peace of stillness within. Even if you only have time for ten minutes of daily meditation, consider how this will help give you peace of mind as your attachment to incessant thinking slowly subsides.

If you are not already meditating on a regular basis, now is the time to put meditation sessions on your daily calendar for the coming week. It's usually best to meditate at the same time each day. Simply jot down the time for meditation and keep the appointment, just as if it were time for an important job interview. In reality, it is the ultimate employment conference for your soul's eternal meeting with the divine.

* Ask your family or friends to remind you to perform your daily meditation.

* Set a timer or an alarm to ring a few minutes prior to your meditation session.

* Make sure you have a quiet place to meditate. Use earplugs, an earmuff-style headset (like construction workers use), or a noise-canceling headset.

* It's best to meditate sitting up (spine straight) in a comfortable position on a cushion on the floor or in a chair.

✳ Try to meditate the same amount of time each day. If meditating for twenty or thirty minutes is too long in the beginning, just start off meditating for ten minutes and slowly increase your time.

✳ Try any of the meditations described in this book or your own favorite meditation.

When you practice meditation on a regular basis, you will be able to dive deeply into the divine peace that lies dormant within your inner body and your mundane sensitivity challenges will pale in comparison. Even if you do not have profound spiritual experiences, meditating lets your consciousness momentarily transcend this temporary Earth plane as you immerse yourself in spirit.

Awakening Your Soul in Nature

*S*pending time in nature can awaken your innate, spiritual qualities. Your highly sensitive nervous system will easily relax when you spend time in the calmness of nature. In an urban environment, it is easy to become deluded, believing that it's natural to sit in traffic jams on freeways, inhale toxic pollution, and listen to sirens, motorcycles, and grating rap music blasting from cars. But when you can be in a natural setting, you realize the calm serenity that waits within you.

Since, as an HSP, you have the capacity to feel joy and appreciate beauty deeply, you can instantaneously enter into a tranquil state when you spend time in a lovely natural environment. Your soul spontaneously soars upward toward a divine state as you gaze deeply at the delicate forms of white clouds floating in the unfathomable blue sky, or when you stroll along a park trail savoring the beauty of a bluebird or inhaling the delicate fragrance of a cornucopia of multicolored flowers.

Plan regular visits to a natural environment this week. Some examples of places to relax in nature are:

✳ Going to your local park

✳ Gardening

✳ Spending time at a lake, a river, or the ocean

✳ Going on a hike in the woods

✳ Spending a weekend at a cabin in a rural setting

✳ Visiting an orchard or nursery

✳ Watching the sunrise or sunset

Remember that in a bucolic natural environment, you can feel your connection to the divine more deeply.

Conclusion

*C*ongratulations! You have just completed fifty-two exercises that have helped you cope with our overstimulating world. However, remember that your practice of creating inner peace is an ongoing process. It would be beneficial to choose the areas in your life that are the most challenging for you and repeat those related exercises on a regular basis each week. This is the perfect time to review the relevant exercises and note on your calendar when you plan to repeat each technique.

As you keep practicing the weekly exercises in this book, you will continue to experience more joy and tranquility in your life. Remember that you are not alone. There are millions of highly sensitive people in every country who are also trying to cope with a sensitive nervous system. Share some of the helpful methods that you have learned in this book with your

HSP and non-HSP friends, family, and coworkers. Equipped with your new survival skills, you can now serve as a beacon of light for others trying to navigate through our fastpaced, overstimulating world.

My best wishes are with you for a life filled with good health, inner peace, and joy. Please visit my Web site, www .hspsurvival.com, for more information, and please feel free to contact me with any questions.

Ted Zeff, Ph.D., received his doctorate in psychology in 1981 from the California Institute of Integral Studies in San Francisco, CA. He currently teaches workshops on coping techniques for highly sensitive people. He has taught stress reduction and insomnia management for more than fifteen years at various hospitals and medical groups. He is author of *The Highly Sensitive Person's Survival Guide*. Please visit his Web site, **www.hspsurvival.com.**